JANUS

Best wishes to my sister [illegible] Antonina Bellesarte,

Frank Salvatore

Hodson
_30/6/07_

JANUS

Frank Salvatore

Word Association Publishers
205 Fifth Avenue
Tarentum, Pennsylvania 15084

ISBN: 1-932205-62-4
Library of Congress Control Number: 2003108713

Word Association Publishers
205 Fifth Avenue
Tarentum, Pennsylvania 15084
www.wordassociation.com

To

Grace Ricci Salvatore

Vibrant and beautiful, quiet and unpretentious, she was the guiding force in our family, the one who opened our eyes to love. Her voyage in life was simple yet elegant, and deeply Christian. Her belief in God was her vehicle to Heaven and ours to earthly peace.

Life without her is suddenly complex, less virtuous, touched with melancholy. And yet we draw comfort knowing that she is with us still in our daughter, Linda, and our son Richard.

I cannot articulate the love that she gave us, but I know it was infinite.

The
Salvato-Ceppone Family Tree

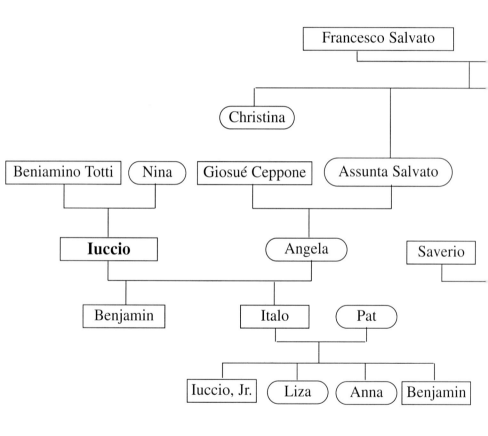

Francesco Salvato

Christina

Beniamino Totti — Nina — Giosué Ceppone — Assunta Salvato

Iuccio — Angela — Saverio

Benjamin — Italo — Pat

Iuccio, Jr. — Liza — Anna — Benjamin

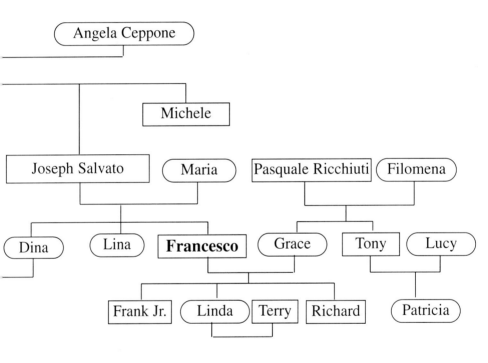

Foreword

Frank Salvatore's *Janus* is a story that can be enjoyed as both history and love story by Italian and American readers alike.

The book begins with a love story, one that could take place only in Italy. Iuccio Totti is a passionate young fascist whose vociferous praise of *Il Duce*'s antics has paid off in the form of a leadership role within the movement. And then Iuccio falls in love with and marries a local damsel who knows nothing of the politics of his small town, having been born in America.

Iuccio's gradual transformation from fascist hard-liner to skeptic is masterfully described, as is his increasing awareness upon becoming involved in the Spanish Civil War that he has fought in the wrong war and espoused the wrong cause. Many Italians who had ardently participated in the fascist dream found themselves equally disappointed. American readers will learn the truth about a period that has been sadly neglected by Italian and American historians.

Italian readers, on the other hand, may take a special interest in the struggles of Frank and his family when they, like many other Italians, immigrated to the New World. Much ink has been expended to elucidate the plight of Italian immigrants, especially of those who arrived on American soil at the turn of the century and who, lacking the rudiments of education, had to accept the most menial jobs. Frank's case is different. He arrived at the end of World War II, with a fairly good education that should have allowed him under normal circumstances to get decent employment. But a subtle anti-Italian sentiment was present among the intelligentsia with whom Frank came in contact. Even though Frank had attended an American college and held the rank of officer in the United States Army, the principal of an Ohio high school refused to give him employment, simply because Frank was of Italian descent.

Frank was to encounter two types of Americans: the callous, bigoted type, such as the principal described above, and the noble, idealistic type, such as his teachers, who imparted to him the knowledge of all that is sacred in the American political system. The contrast between these two forces sharpened Frank's view of America. He saw, on the one hand, the nobility of the great American experiment and felt a great attachment to his new homeland. He could not, however, ignore the many ironies evident in a country that preached liberty yet practiced discrimination. *Janus* is essentially the story of Frank's struggle to understand this great, flawed country of ours, and readers who follow him in this struggle will gain a fresh perspective on American social studies.

Frank would never have written *Janus* without the inspiration of his beloved muse, his late wife, Grace, who was at his side from the time they met in high school. He has dedicated the book to her, rightfully so, for her presence can be felt on every page. No more fitting tribute could be paid to her than the gift of Frank's memories so lovingly detailed in this book.

Robert C. Melzi, Ph.D.
Professor Emeritus
Distinguished Scholar
Widener University

Preface

As these pages evolved, I began to feel like Janus himself. Like the god with two faces, I was a man with two selves, being both Italian and American. As a young man of nineteen, I had abandoned Italy for America. Mine is therefore a journey of contrasts, a struggle to understand the dual nature of my adopted homeland and the people of *E Pluribus Unum*. America was an enigma. It was complicated and equivocal, but more tolerant and compassionate than any other country in the world.

The idea to share my story with others dates back to 1947, just after the end of World War II. Writing about my life seemed like a strange idea at the time, because there were so many bitter experiences I wanted to forget. However, as time passed, I began to look on those same experiences with nostalgia, and I was compelled to write of poverty, hunger, oppression, and the nightmare of an uncertain future. Like Alfieri, the great Italian poet, who said, "I wanted, I always wanted, I strongly wanted," writing, for me, became an obsession.

I give you a story about the dynamism of immigrants, about good and evil, about freedom and prejudice, about the power of persistence and love. And this story is set against a harsh background of reality—fascism, war, and industrial America.

I have written this story for several reasons. The first is purely selfish—to leave my children, Linda and Richard, a bit of myself, their link to the traditions, language, and culture of the country to which they can trace their roots. The other is to honor the great women in my life—my mother, a fearless woman who represented the goodness of Italy, and my wife, Grace, whose gentle wisdom guided me in the struggle to find the goodness of America.

Acknowledgments

While the book speaks from the heart, it would not have been possible without the contribution of many friends. However, there are a few who deserve to be singled out.

I am especially grateful to Dr. Robert Melzi, Professor Emeritus at Widener University, distinguished scholar and linguist, my teacher, colleague and friend for almost a half-century, who gave me much-needed guidance; Dr. Richard Juliani, Professor of Sociology at Villanova University, who offered generous support; Laura Ulmer, Jack Rybnick and John Edelman, teachers of English who were my colleagues for twenty-six years and who read the typescript and offered inestimable assistance in this long journey of mine.

Special thanks to my cousin Joseph Tatta and friend Anna Forte, for their input, and to my indefatigable editor, Nan Newell, for her patience and gentleness.

Finally, I would be remiss if I did not express my love for my wife, Grace, and my children, Linda and Richard, and my gratitude for their abiding faith in me.

1 In the city of Campobasso, the feast of *Corpus Domini* is celebrated in a special way, unique in the world, different from that of other cities in Italy. From the first of the year, the city prepares for the feast's highlight, a live representation of the *Dodici Misteri* (Twelve Mysteries), an event that has deep religious roots in most of Europe. It reproduces the live miracles of saints and martyrs, and addresses the mysteries of Heaven and Hell, birth and death, and the immortality of our souls. In Campobasso this secular tradition has its roots in the eighteenth century.

In 1740 Paolo Di Zinno made some changes to his new forged-metal devices, allowing live characters to parade throughout the city of Campobasso, suspended in the air above the floats. This religious spectacle has since excited the whole province, which comes in large groups for the occasion.

The representation of the Mysteries on June 2, 1930, was exceptional. The sky was clear and the air was fresh as the multitude gathered on both sides of the street. In fact, the weather was so beautiful that the crowd reached a number never seen before. That year's celebration was also exceptional for the competition that existed among all the participants, some of whom paid large sums to be chosen as angels, saints, or devils for the final representation of the Twelve Mysteries. It was indeed an unusual year. For the first time in the history of the Mysteries, the role of Lucifer went to a nonresident of the city, a certain Iuccio Totti from Toro.

His personification of the Devil was so believable that he created a panic among the children. His long tongue resembled a snake coming out of a hole, and his white, pointed teeth contrasted with his lamp-blackened face, enough to offend the devils themselves. Iuccio had a diabolical voice, and when he recited certain sentences, he had the power to terrify:

JANUS

Tunzella, tunzella, vietenne, vietenne, a la sigetta r'ora, acchiapete a sta coda. (Little girl, little girl, come, come to this golden chair, hold on to this tail.)

While Iuccio was repeating *"tunzella, tunzella,"* his eyes were fixed on a girl, and hers on him, as if both were hypnotized. Neither was able to stop looking at the other. It was as if they had been drawn together by an invisible force that permeated their bodies and immobilized them, until the girl's mother realized what was going on and hastened to take her away in order to stop the Devil's bewitchment. The sinister refrain *"tunzella, tunzella"* continued to be heard by the crowd, and that echo continued to follow mother and daughter even after they had left town.

The elders of the city could not remember a Lucifer who had represented Hell so well. In fact, on that day, all the eyes that normally would have admired the Eleven Mysteries were fixed on the Twelfth, on this devilish man. Everyone was stunned that a man not of that city could speak their dialect so perfectly. When he disappeared at the end of the parade, rumors circulated that Iuccio had supernatural powers.

Who was he? Where did he come from? Who were his parents?

A few days later, one of the senior citizens present, Uncle Giulio Di Giulio, with a mustache resembling the horns of a Texan cow, took his cane and tied his horse to the cart. Being a collector of sheepskins, and pretending to go to one of his customers, he set out for Iuccio's village, to uncover Iuccio's past and satisfy his own curiosity.

He learned that Iuccio was a hothead, and rebellious. As a child, Iuccio did not yield to authority, physical punishment, or humiliation and had already developed a hard, aggressive, and domineering personality.

He also learned that Iuccio was familiar with the Devil. One winter night, with some friends, he had proposed to do spiritualism. Something went wrong in that experiment, because it seemed that the end of the world had come. Witnesses told

Uncle Giulio that from this diabolical experiment came a very strong wind that blew off the roof tiles all over the village. Then, miraculously, all returned to normal the day after.

For a long time people talked of this strange happening. Giovanni Serpo, Iuccio's most faithful friend, wanted to prevent Iuccio from taking the secret to his grave. For posterity's sake, Giovanni asked him for the formula for such an audacious enterprise, but neither he nor anyone else succeeded in getting it. Iuccio wanted to be the first one to go to Hell, in the other world, and be able to come back alive to tell everyone about his infernal experiences.

Uncle Giulio became very curious and wanted to know more. From Mr. Felice, Iuccio's elementary school teacher, the mustached old man learned that one drizzly afternoon, Iuccio, returning from school where he was enrolled in the second grade, was very nervous because the teacher had pulled his ears for his mischievousness earlier that day. He hated school for the physical punishment and humiliation that he had to endure. He had hardly reached home when he became even more agitated because he could not find the two anchovies that his mother had left for him to eat that afternoon.

When the poor grandmother told him that Trouble the cat had eaten the anchovies, Iuccio immediately began to pound the floor with his left foot, wanting to punish it, as if the floor, and not the cat, had committed the culinary crime. Then he threatened his grandmother, saying that he would burn down the house if she did not retrieve the anchovies that the greedy cat had eaten. The desperate grandmother had to borrow some anchovies from a neighbor to placate him. Nothing more was ever heard about Trouble.

Another time, a woman teacher hit Iuccio on his left hand, even though he was left-handed, so that he could not write with that hand. Iuccio took the wooden stick from her and hit the poor teacher on the head. Pandemonium erupted in the classroom. All of his companions applauded him. They jumped on the desks and created such a disorder that teachers from other rooms hastened to rescue their unfortunate colleague and re-establish order. From then on Iuccio became the leader of all the students. He was just seven years old.

2 Iuccio's rebellious behavior worried his mother who, small and sickly, was growing old prematurely. Beniamino, her husband, had gone to the United States, but before leaving, had given her specific orders. Their son should receive a good education and grow up to be a good Christian. They knew the sayings "He who lives by the sword dies by it" and "Love conquers love," and they provided him with an environment of comforts, trying to avoid the parental severity that was commonly imposed on peasant children.

They lived in a villa that his father had bought from a baron. For them it was a kind of social promotion. People had even grown accustomed to calling Iuccio's mother "Madam Nina" as a sign of respect for Beniamino's economic progress. Iuccio considered himself refined and elitist, but the people despised him for his arrogance, especially when he became of age and started to run around through the village on his new motorcycle, scaring the horses and donkeys of the farmers entering the village at night.

The first-grade teachers had assured Madam Nina that her son was vivacious and intelligent. However, she knew him well and was not convinced that she would be capable of guiding her rebellious son on the right path by herself.

In fact, Iuccio had to repeat third grade because of his temerity. Yet, in spite of his uncontrollable behavior, he had the respect of almost all his companions and even some teachers, who liked him for his shrewdness and admired his reputation as the best of the *Balilla*, the youngest fascist pioneers. When fascist instructions were given, he finished first in every competition. When he became leader of his squad, his commands were clear and precise, and all followed him without making mistakes.

At the end of the year, his superiors appraised all the *Balilla*. Iuccio always scored the highest; during the summer, he was the first in the region to be sent to Rome for paramilitary training. Here he had the opportunity to see for the first time the beauties of imperial Rome.

The city of the Caesars opened his eyes and provided the incentive that would make him a model fascist. Among the wonders of the ancient *Caput Mundi*, Rome, he also visited the vast St. Peter's Basilica. His priest, Don Camillo, always cautioned him about the difficulty in going to Heaven. So as not to offend the Lord, Iuccio started to genuflect at every altar, even though there were so many. Turning his eyes to the sky, he begged God to see him in His big sacred temple. Then, aiming his hand toward the north, and then toward the south, the east and the west, he made the sign of the cross and left Saint Peter's church.

Of the many facets of his personality as a young man, two were salient. In his paramilitary life he was obsessed with following all the rules, whereas in civilian life he was adventurous, anarchical, and indolent. He loved *la dolce vita*, the sweetness of a careless life. He was always the first to the late-evening dinners, banquets, and dances.

He did not care how hard his father worked to save some money in America, nor did he realize how frugally his mother lived in order to provide all the comforts for him. The future did not worry him. He had done little to earn the middle-school diploma that could have led to a job. But the desire to work was never part of his personal philosophy. Work was for others.

At that time, the people were indoctrinated to believe that Italy was strong and great, a worthy heiress of ancient Rome. Fascism was a dominant ideology in 1930, and nobody dared to stop it, neither socialists nor communists, nor King Victor Emanuele himself.

The man of the hour was called *Il Duce*, and was revered as a god. He was the only one who could resolve the problems of Italy. At least this was the perception. After all, was it not he who had destroyed the Mafia? Was it not he who had opened the schools to all the Italian children, schools that before had educated only the children of the rich? The whole world knew that Italy's trains now departed and arrived on time. Fascism had brought the country a social stability and pride that it had not experienced since Roman times.

3 The Fascist National Party gave many young people hope, promising them the world. Only a few were not members, and Iuccio threatened anyone who opposed its ideology. He enjoyed speaking to large crowds and quickly became the most tenacious propagandist and the leader of the fascist movement of his village, finding in fascism the road to an easy career.

Iuccio was one of a few who could afford to buy a radio, and he listened to it constantly to keep well informed about everything that was happening in Italy and abroad. He listened attentively to all the speeches by prominent fascists and especially to those of the *Duce*. When there was no one in the house, he would practice giving speeches, looking at himself in the mirror, making faces as an actor, imitating his god, the *Duce*.

He was so animated that one day his mother, coming home unexpectedly, found him pretending to be speaking to a fascist assembly, explaining the fascist gospel to those people who, according to him, had not yet been baptized into this new religion.

The village where he lived, Toro, sits on a hill on which the church of Saint Salvatore had been built as if to dominate and protect the valley of the Tappino River. From the bell tower of the church, one can see all the neighboring villages. To the west, far away, are the Matese Mountains. The medieval streets from the north to the south are narrow and long, connected by short ones from the east to the west.

One day, while Iuccio was giving a speech before one of

those fascist gatherings under that imposing bell tower, he saw among the crowd a girl who looked very different from the other village girls. First of all, her clothes were different. But beyond that, she was delicate, with long, curly blond hair and rosy cheeks. She seemed to emanate a scent of roses. Her eyelashes were like those of a doll. As soon as he saw her, he did something uncharacteristic: he shortened his speech, which, during that fascist period, would normally have lasted for hours. He recognized the girl on whom his eyes had fixed on that June 2, day of the Mysteries, and who, from then on, appeared every night in his dreams.

He ended his speech with the usual "Mussolini is always right," "Long live the *Duce*," and "Power to us!"

Now he felt sure of what he was doing and said to himself, "As a fascist, I have done my duty for the day and I am now free to do what I want." His heart, however, at that moment, was something other than purely fascist. He was so spellbound by the face of this young girl that the Fascist Party suddenly became secondary despite his oath to it.

4 In 1929, because of the Depression in America, Giosué Ceppone had decided to go back to Toro with his wife, Assunta, and his daughter, Angela, who seemed as beautiful as an angel. She was the young girl to whom Iuccio was drawn, even though she was only fourteen years old. This day she looked very attractive in a white-and-blue dress, with stars on the back collar like a sailor's, and white shoes— evidence of a rich background. In the past, Iuccio had pretty much had his way, and he was now determined to meet her.

Finally, some days later, while Angela was going through the streets of the historic district of the village, Iuccio met her and tried to speak to her. But the girl did not understand one iota of Italian, except for some dialect. When Angela returned home, she, being a good girl, reported the incident to her mother, who immediately became suspicious. That whole night Assunta could not close her eyes, because Angela could not identify the man. Doubts came to her mind as to whether she had made the right decision in returning to her native land. But as the days passed in that euphoric climate of parades and celebrations, Assunta and her husband seemed more reassured, almost forgetting the incident.

On April 21, the Fascist Party commemorated the birth of Rome with a big parade. On such occasions, under the shade of the bell tower, Iuccio always delivered a speech. This day he began his speech with "Long live the *Duce!*" and then continued: "Comrade townsmen, since the fall of the Roman Empire, we have been enslaved by foreign oppressors and lords. Not even the insurrections and sacrifices of the 1850s gave us freedom. We, innocent and exploited by the rich, have been abused for well over fifteen hundred years. Even during our most glorious period, the Renaissance, foreigners dominated us, oppressing us not only economically, but also culturally.

"There will be no more 'laws of the first night' to violate our women. Fascism has given us back our dignity, which the nobles stole from us. The *Duce* has given us back our power, which was usurped by the aristocracy. There will be no more injustices against the poor. Mussolini has finally reunited the state and the Church with the Lateran Treaty, giving full liberty to all Catholics and other religious groups. All the civilized countries admire him; he is the envy of the world. Today all is clear to us. Exact limits exist between good and evil, between vice and virtue, between right and wrong. With work, with faith in the *Duce* and faith in God, we will throw out the leeches of our society, the servants and the cowards. No longer will we live under the yoke of servitude."

With this last sentence, the crowd became euphoric, applauding for a long time. It was then that Angela pointed her finger toward the young fascist, saying, "Mother, that's the man who wanted to speak to me." Assunta immediately translated this for her sister-in-law.

"He is lazy, and arrogant," Maria answered.

Poor Assunta. Her first suspicion confirmed, she took Angela by the hand and walked toward her house, followed by her sister in-law.

That evening, while they were at home with many other family members, they talked about problems, about Iuccio's desire to talk to Angela. Each one spoke his mind, without Angela's understanding anything. The conclusion was clear: there was nothing serious enough to worry about.

Michelangelo, Angela's nicest uncle and a man at peace with himself, said, "You, dear sister-in-law, have to understand that the village has not changed for years. It is today as when you left it, despite the progress. Here we have not had a crime since the time of Gilio Gialone, the brigand who made us all tremble at the beginning of the twentieth century. There are only two thousand souls living here, just as you left them. The girl is safe to go anywhere, because nothing ever happens in our village. Today, with this new regime, you can send Angela alone on the train from Palermo to Milan, without anyone molesting her. In fact, Mussolini has completely destroyed the Mafia in Sicily, which nobody had succeeded in doing before him—not even Prime Minister Crispi himself, who was Sicilian."

It was obvious, even to the new arrivals, that law and order had replaced violence. With Michelangelo's comforting words, Assunta felt that she did not have to worry anymore and could allow Angela some leeway in her associations.

Angela, curious about all this attention from the stranger, asked her only girlfriend and cousin, "How come that young man tips his hat and smiles at me when he sees me?"

"It is only a sign of respect," her cousin Francesca replied.

For Angela, the long summer days passed quickly. All her friends wanted to play with her, because they were amused by her strange way of speaking. She enjoyed wandering through the historic streets of the village. In the evenings she was spellbound, listening to the choir of the crickets and chasing lightning bugs up to where the streets got lost in the darkness of the fields.

Her contemporaries, attracted by her exotic, well-developed figure and mature manners, sought her company. Her relatives considered her their princess; they often took her with them to the fields to harvest and thresh the wheat. To amuse her, they put her on a perforated iron platform pulled by horses threshing the ears of the wheat.

Life was one continuous vacation. But Angela continued to think about America, her girlfriends, her school. Even though she had made some friends, it was difficult for her to grow accustomed to their medieval ways.

One day in August she was awakened by an explosion: the village was celebrating the feast day of the patron saint. Tradition held that the holiday begin in the morning with fireworks. The big burst frightened the poor girl. Thinking that terrible things were about to happen, she ran into her parents' bedroom for protection. "These are things that happen during a celebration," explained her mother.

Later, the church bells started to toll, forcing her to cover her ears, which were unaccustomed to so much noise. Then the band marched through the village, making beautiful music to uplift the people's mood. Angela was to experience these occasions frequently.

5 The whole summer passed, and Angela made much progress in learning Italian. Between the national and the religious holidays, Iuccio became more and more visible to Angela, until finally she began to smile back at him. Meanwhile, Iuccio did not pass up any opportunity to see her. He was always polite and kind to her family whenever he now encountered them, even though he had never been so before. Socially, the Ceppone family was a step below his.

The young fascist's plans were starting to bear fruit, and

he was plotting the best way to tell her that he wanted to speak to her at all costs. His eyes followed her everywhere without ever arousing suspicion. Finally, he found his chance. In the first week of September, there was a soccer game, which half of the villagers attended. Angela, encouraged by her cousin Francesca, also went to see this competition, one of the few spectacles in the area.

This soccer field seemed shabby to the American girl, accustomed to green American fields, cheerleaders in fashionable uniforms rooting for their team, and marching bands. Here the grass did not grow, because boys always played there, trampling the young grass while it was growing, never giving it a chance to reach maturity. Under a centimeter of surface there was *tufa,* a finer rock. Even after a downpour, all that one could see was bone-dry dirt with stones. The ground was good only for making bricks.

Then Angela remembered that in America it was Labor Day, a big national holiday that marked the start of the football season.

Iuccio approached her, inviting her and Francesca to take a walk with him. Fortunately, the public was so involved in the game that no one noticed them as they left. Cousin Francesca served as a shield, because, while they walked along the main road, Iuccio gave the impression that he was interested in her, not Angela.

When they finally reached a place where nobody was able to see or hear them, Iuccio revealed his infinite love for Angela. She answered him with only an enigmatic smile. Then he thanked Francesca and begged her as he would a Madonna to meet him at the next soccer event and play along with him as he pretended to be in love with her and not Angela.

For Iuccio this love had to remain a secret, since he feared Angela's father, who was known to be an obstinate fellow. Giosué was tall and strong, and during the First World War had fought for America on the French front, where had distinguished himself as a very brave soldier. He had been decorated with the Congressional Medal of Honor, the highest medal conferred on a soldier. At the end of that world conflict, before returning to America, he had revisited his native village, where he had been received as a hero. Since then the people called him "the Sergeant."

It was obvious to everybody that Iuccio was changing: his new behavior, serious and responsible, caused people in the village to start talking about him in a different way. His companions noticed that he did not participate in the fascist gatherings as he once did. Stranger yet was his attitude toward church, which he began to attend on Sundays—the ten o'clock mass, when he was sure to see her.

Completely contrary to his character, he went from being a wild horse to a tamed one. Only a month ago, surrendering to a woman would have been a threat to his manhood and to his fascist, ideological superiority. What had happened? Where was the discipline for which he had earned so much respect?

He was so much in love that in his heart he renamed her Mona Lisa, certainly for her beautiful face, but also because she put on a mysterious face—an enigmatic, elusive smile like that of *La Gioconda*—whenever people spoke to her, as she understood very little Italian.

The two saw each other secretly. Their love was like a volcano ready to explode at any moment. Iuccio was not accustomed to being perceived by his friends as losing control of himself. For years Iuccio had had neither heart nor soul. His friends called him Casanova for his behavior toward his lady friends. His eyes were like x-rays, regarding females with meticulousness. But his loving behavior toward Angela was genuine. She was different from all the others, delicate and beautiful as a flower, a rose that would never fade. He wanted to be the one to protect her. She was becoming his whole life. On his twentieth birthday, he decided to propose marriage to her.

Angela was under age and a lot younger than he, but as a sensible young woman, she let him know that her parents would never consent to such a marriage proposal and she begged him to wait for the right time. By now it was his heart, not his head, controlling his destiny. Usually, once he made up his mind, nobody ever succeeded in changing it.

The words *surrender, wait, have patience* had never been part of his vocabulary. Audaciously he planned a detailed escape that would not arouse suspicion. At first Angela rejected his proposal to run away with him, because disobeying her parents was not part of her character. She begged him to wait for the propitious moment.

Contrary to her normally calm demeanor, she had now become irritable and restless; she felt too controlled, unable to do what she wanted. She considered herself a prisoner. This way of living suffocated her. The only things that comforted her were her dreams. She remembered with nostalgia her childhood in America when in the summer, with her girlfriends in her little town, she would go bicycling for miles on country roads flanked by wheat and corn that farmers had sowed in November and March.

She remembered the walks to the ice cream parlor where, with the same girlfriends, she would pass the time talking about certain boys or teachers and then laughing, joking like rascals, having a great time and dreaming of their rosy future. Every Friday afternoon in autumn, they would go to see their school's football games. On Saturday evening they would go to the movies, and finally on Sunday afternoon they would listen to their favorite broadcasts on radio.

Now she was embittered in this village that seemed like a cage, and although she loved her parents, she felt trapped by them. She cried when she was alone, finding comfort only in the man who had declared unconditional love for her. She needed this love to ease her sufferings and her loneliness.

Iuccio was a good psychologist. One sinister look of his was enough to subdue people. Therefore, in their last secret meeting he wanted to be sure of himself. With his know-how he hypnotized her, asking her for her eternal love.

"Yes, I shall love you for the rest of my life," she swore;

and when she came out of this artificial sleep, still dazed, she caved in to his renewed exhortation with a silent, strong "yes," embracing and kissing him, promising a love for him that not even death would end.

6 It was spring again and already the warm sun caressed and penetrated one's bones. One needed only to look around to realize the rejuvenation of nature, awakened again and garlanded with flowers, as if it wanted to welcome and facilitate the plans for the two lovers.

Iuccio was ready for this adventure. To him it was worth any consequence, even if it lasted only one night with the risk of ending up in jail, even if it should end his political career to which he had devoted so much energy. The *Duce*'s mottoes came to mind: "It is better to live one day like a lion than one hundred like a sheep" and "Work dignifies man." This last one bothered him a little, because he had never worked and he was still living on his father's money. But now the only thing that mattered to him was eloping.

On the night before they were to leave, he instructed her when and where to meet in the early hours of the following morning, repeating his plans more than once to make sure she understood. Then they parted. He went to the city to buy train tickets. Then he returned to the village, passing Angela's balcony, which faced the road leading out of the village toward the city.

At 2:30 A.M. on that fateful April night, Angela, with a racing heart, jumped easily from the balcony into Bianchino's two-horse carriage. Bianchino, so called for having whitish hair since birth, was the only one in the village willing to help them to elope. Fortunately, on the road there was not even a dog, and the two escaped without being seen.

Bianchino asked her to lie down in the lowest part of the wagon and then covered her with a blanket. One kilometer out of the village, Iuccio was waiting for her, next to the soccer field where they had met for the first time with Francesca. He climbed into the carriage while she remained covered, almost under his feet. Neither one had brought a suitcase; they had only a few liras and personal documents.

About two kilometers farther, a crossroad led to the villages of Campodipietra and St. Giovanni in Galdo. Two policemen patrolling the area stopped them and asked Iuccio and the coachman for documents. Iuccio, with much indifference, showed them the P.N.F., the National Fascist Party ID card, saying that he was on his way to catch the train for Rome. They were allowed to move on. When they arrived at the station, they had to wait a few minutes before taking the train for Termoli, which went east instead west. Iuccio had intentionally misled the militiamen in order to confuse any pursuers.

The sky was so clear that one could almost touch the stars. Instead, the stars touched the young lovers. At exactly 3:30, they left the city. The strategy to avoid suspicion was to travel apart from each other, Angela sitting next to a woman and Iuccio a few seats behind.

7 In the spring, nature in this area is very pleasant to the eyes, introducing a colorful rural panorama of sainfoin, Spanish broom, and wild flowers whose fragrance can reach the houses in the village. Time goes by very slowly, and when one is in tune with nature and its environment, one enjoys it in all its aspects. It is especially enjoyable for those who are free from work.

On this morning Assunta got up a little late, about eight o'clock and not at six as was her custom in the United States. A few minutes later, she passed her daughter's room and noticed that the bed was empty. She looked everywhere but did not find her daughter. Immediately she awoke her husband, who calmly went out into the village, confident that he would find his daughter in some relative's house. But nobody had seen her.

Giosué had the patience of Job, but at that point he began to worry.

Upon returning home, he found some relatives consoling his wife, who was panic-stricken and shouting in vain, "Poor daughter of mine!" From time to time Assunta would pull her hair and hit her head against the wall, cursing at her husband for having returned to Italy, when it was she who had encouraged him to come back. It was true that things in America were going from bad to worse during the Great Depression of 1929, but as a veteran of the First World War, Giosué could always have found some employment. Since nobody had forced her to go back to Italy, Assunta felt so guilty that she continued to pull her hair and bite her arms, as if going mad, until her husband took matters into his own hands. He slapped her on the face to bring her out of her hysteria, and when she fainted, he asked the relatives to look after her. Then he proceeded to the police station.

The chief of police, a tall, strong man of indisputable professionalism, had just gotten up when Giosué arrived. The chief immediately tried to get some information from him and then from some other people in the village.

Just at that time, Iuccio's virtuous mother, thin and fragile, returning from an early mass at the monastery, saw Mr. Ceppone with the police. Hearing what had transpired, she found the courage to tell the officer that her son had run out of the house in the first hours of the morning. The chief wasted no time in notifying all the neighboring police stations to block all the roads leading to Rome, Naples, and Termoli. Then he went to the Ceppones for more information.

The echoes of "poor daughter of mine" were being heard only by Assunta's relatives, because most of the villagers were in church to honor the young Antoinette Tromba and Adriano Bengiamino, about to be united in matrimony after seven years of courtship. The religious ceremony was brief, after which all followed the newlyweds to the square, where, with some family members, they climbed into the carriages to go to a small restaurant.

Meanwhile, the Ceppones' house was full of relatives trying to distract Assunta by talking about the wedding in progress, the bride's outfit, the dowry received. All this trivial talk increased Assunta's anxiety. She mumbled to herself, as if in a deep crisis: "How is this all going to end?" Her heart was broken, just thinking of the shame that this ugly situation could bring upon all of them. Her anxiety was choking her.

At dusk the police chief knocked on the Ceppones' door. As soon as he entered, he reassured everybody that the two fugitives had been apprehended and that they were in good hands in Termoli's jail. Calm was soon restored on Mrs. Ceppone's face, whose eyes were dry because they could no longer produce any tears. After supper, everyone went back home; however, shaken by the bad news of the day, no one was able to sleep.

Early next morning, all the relatives were ready to go to Termoli to the police station, when the chief of police appeared on the doorstep with bad news. There had been a gross misunderstanding. The prisoners were not Angela and Iuccio, but Adriano Bengiamino and Antoinette Tromba, the newlyweds. These two, after the celebration at the restaurant, had left the village that same day, and they were now angry for not having been able to consummate their marriage. For the Ceppone family, this accursed false trail, yielding no trace of their daughter, jolted them again.

In the meantime the fugitives had succeeded in eluding the police roadblocks and were on the train to Pescara. Iuccio let Angela sit in front of everybody in a coach, again sitting a little behind her and telling her to pretend to sleep. But the poor girl, tired as she was, with her nerves consuming her, fell into a deep sleep and began mumbling foreign words. Iuccio immediately understood the danger. Pretending to go to the toilet, he passed by her and woke her up.

As soon as they arrived at Pescara station, they left the train. He told her not to utter a single word for fear that her accent would reveal her true identity.

JANUS

8 After a few days of anxiety and worry in the Ceppones' house, the relatives did not know what course of action to take. They wanted to do something for the sake of Angela's innocent soul, especially to avoid a scandal in their family, because the rumors were spreading quickly. But what should they do? Uncle Michelangelo suggested that, without letting anyone in the village know their plans, they should go to their farms to look for the girl there. It was possible that the pair was hidden in one of them.

As if they had finally found the solution, each one, excited by the uncle's plan, left the village by a different route. The chief of police, in a sign of respect for Uncle Michelangelo, only shook his head a couple of times to indicate his lack of approval for such an endeavor. Even though the chief recognized that his efforts had been in vain, he told them that only the law sooner or later would solve their problem.

Assunta was in a terrible state of mind, blaming herself for removing Angela from the only world she had known. She thought endlessly about how Angela, in America, had been a model daughter. In school she had always received good grades, and the teachers had always praised her for being a perfect student. Before departing for Italy, Angela had cried day and night because she did not want to leave her little dog, Dukie, that she had re-named Duchino, the little prince. As a little girl, she had secretly sworn eternal love to him.

Assunta's mind was full of these memories of the past; and she would look up into the sky, reciting the mea culpa. At night she could not sleep; insomnia drove her crazy. Not even Giosué, her husband, could sleep, and the two argued about who had really decided to go back to Italy. These squabbles lasted for hours.

9 In thc village the news leaked out and people started talking about it. It was hay-harvesting time, and a lot of farmers were singing refrains, among which was one recently written about the Ceppone tragicomedy:

> *Angela, beautiful Angela*
> *who flies like a swallow*
> *into the cage of Marianico'.*
> *Hurry up, hurry up*
> *into Bianchino's carriage.*

Marianico', Iuccio's cousin, was angered by this accusation and explained that she had never helped Iuccio escape with Angela. She admitted only to having delivered a letter from Iuccio some weeks earlier in which he spoke of his insane love for Angela.

After the fourth day, this drama seemed about to be resolved. Iuccio had sent a telegram to his Uncle Peppone, promising their return if the Ceppones would consent to their marriage. If things did not go according to his plans, he would not forgive God Himself.

This irresponsible action worried Angela's parents, who immediately gathered the whole family for suggestions. After various animated scenes, all was concluded in a positive way that avoided a tragedy, scandal, or embarrassment. The two families assumed the responsibility and the obligations.

Spontaneously, yet quietly, Assunta said, "One can't squeeze the chicken's neck to squeeze the eggs out of her. I would like to kill him, but he will be my son-in-law."

She had always protected her daughter and held high her dreams for Angela's wedding, possibly with a prince, because she had raised her as a princess. She had imagined a sumptuous wedding reception in a big restaurant, like those she had sometimes attended in America. Unfortunately, it seemed that her dream had eroded like a castle in the sand, leaving only hurt feelings. Now she had to be satisfied with an arrogant young man whose future was a big question mark.

She remembered the joy when Angela took her first step, pronounced her first word, "Mommy," then plunged into her lap. Assunta now thought that only her strong faith in God would make a good situation out of a bad one.

10 At the end of a late spring evening, Bianchino, with the same carriage, brought Iuccio and Angela back to the village, where they were welcomed by both families.

The day after, they were the first at the town hall, where the mayor in front of witnesses declared them husband and wife. Later on, there was a religious ceremony, the couple being recognized, forgiven, and blessed by the Catholic Church in St. Salvatore, where the wedding took place. They arrived there in the same carriage that had helped them run away and were welcomed with the applause of guests and the blessing of Schubert's *Ave Maria*.

He wore a blue suit. She wore a white dress with a white veil, white shoes, and white gloves, and she carried a bouquet of white flowers, to make the customary announcement of her purity.

Upon arriving at the altar, they held each other's hand, seeming nervous, as everybody else seemed to be, especially her parents and his mother. While in church, there were some difficult moments, because the bride, who did not yet understand Italian well, found the priest's words incomprehensible.

It was evident that Father Giacinto, that morning, had spent more time attending to his god Bacchus, that sizzling white wine, than to his rites and religious duties. At that point the bridegroom, who had always been sure of himself in the past, also became excited to the point where he could not put the ring on Angela's finger. But at the moment of truth, each reassured everyone there with a clear and loud "yes," to a long applause from all the people.

At the end of the ceremony, the priest let the bells ring as if, with that signal, he wanted to eliminate any sin that remained between the newlyweds. This amorous story, which had held a whole village in suspense for some weeks, had brought joy to two hearts in bloom with the love of spring.

11

After their wedding trip, an atmosphere of calm descended on the two families, who tried everything to make good come out of what had begun so fraught with emotion.

The families resolved that the young couple would live in the Tottis' house, a bit isolated, just a few meters from the village. For Iuccio, opting to live with his mother-in-law would have meant going to war, because they were like the Devil and holy water. He could not stand the negative questioning from his mother-in-law, who in her heart had not forgiven him for having torn her flower from her prematurely. But both Madam Nina and Assunta were always together to facilitate life for their respective children.

The moral roots of the local traditions are deeply entrenched; they do not forgive any wrongdoing. But Iuccio was such a compelling personality that almost everybody had forgotten his rebellious past. For him everything was returning to normal; as in the past, he had come out of a difficult situation with the elegance of a diplomat. Indeed, he operated faster mentally than the others.

During the first year of marriage, the two hearts plunged deeply into their love. They never left each other except to go to work, and they would suffer a great deal if they had to be separated for any time. They liked their contact so much that they always held hands, like two friends, and they kissed each other continually as if one kiss were sweeter than the other. He was always after her, as was she after him.

In their leisure time they often went to the balcony to look at the cheerful colors of the vineyards and to watch the vine-growers picking grapes, while a light breeze carried the echo of refrains of witty songs. They would admire the dawns, the sunsets, the valleys, the Apennine Mountains toward the west, the woods, the river, and all the neighboring villages. These splendid panoramas on late summer nights would become like so many nativity scenes under an arch of gems where comets would streak through the heavens and then extinguish themselves in the void.

Angela liked the first rays of the sun in the morning striking the windows of the homes in the faraway city. She was sometimes amused by the gigantic early-morning shade cast to the west of the village, up to the Matese Mountains. She enjoyed the sun rising in the sky, decreasing little by little as it reached the center of that small cosmos, after which the shade stopped its course completely.

12 Perhaps a love like theirs had never before existed on the face of our planet. Angela was so happy about the news of their first child that nothing else could have excited her more. Madam Nina and Assunta often spoke about the small one to be born. "Will it be a boy? What if it's a girl?" they would ask each other. Their energies were so united for this big event that, rather than be wrong, one was devoting her energies to getting clothes for a boy, and the other for a girl.

To deal with the birth itself, there were Madam Nina, Assunta, and the midwife, Amandola, who had recently arrived from Fiesole in Tuscany with good professional credentials and reputation. Her ways were kind, and she had a warm, subtly seductive personality.

The birth was difficult. The umbilical cord was wrapped around the neck of the newborn, and only Amandola's ability saved both mother and child. As if nothing had happened, it was the midwife who announced the birth of a beautiful little boy. "What name will you give him?" she asked. Iuccio, who was in the kitchen with other relatives, jumped in the air a couple of meters and joyfully replied, "Benjamin, for my father, who is in America."

Amandola congratulated the parents, shook hands with all the relatives, and departed. All congratulated Iuccio, each lifting the glass of sparkling wine ready for the occasion. Then Assunta said, "It is necessary to say '*Che Dio lo benedica*' (God bless him)," and all followed her suggestion.

Changes came to Iuccio, who had never believed in the power of prayer. He now began in full faith to pray to God to let him always be the man that he had become. He hoped to be a good family man and asked never to let him stop feeling pure love for Angela. This was a test of good character and integrity.

The midwife, so as not to alarm anyone, especially Angela, had not said a word, but Amandola worried about the consequences of the umbilical cord around the newborn's neck. She decided to visit the Totti family occasionally just to observe the infant. Without arousing suspicions, she would ask the same question, to which Angela would answer, "Well, very well." Then Angela would continue to elaborate. "He is so active, and he begins to raise himself up with his hands, and then he lifts his head as if to show me how strong he is."

These answers were music to the ears of the midwife. They were the confirmation that Benjamin was growing normally. But Iuccio, who had retained vestiges of his old impertinent and seductive character, misinterpreted these visits, thinking that he was the true reason for her frequent visits.

13 Benjamin was baptized with the honors of a prince. Relatives and neighbors all wanted to hold him, but the new mother seized every opportunity to do so, touching him, kissing him softly, cuddling him, enfolding his little body in her warm arms, as if she were jealous of anyone touching him. When he cried, she would repeat affectionately the motherly refrain that would put him to sleep:

Benjamin, little Benjamin
Beautiful little lover
You are daddy's Benjamin
Mommy's little flower.

All were impressed and amazed at Angela's maternal preparation. Always happy, she had learned from her mother-in-law the culinary art. She had also learned how to iron and sew, making all the articles of clothing and pursuing other domestic matters as if she had been born in that environment. She gained the respect of many women who had at first considered her immature.

Gossip is the most powerful force in the world. It was going around, but it did not interest Angela. She knew well that gossipers can be found in every environment. For instance, someone had derided her openly for her strange language that was not typical of a person as well educated as she. She made childish errors, as often happens with newly arrived immigrants in America who have difficulty with pronunciation, substituting words such as "leave" for "live" and "bitch" for "beech." When Angela spoke about her husband, she called him her "ROM-e-o" instead of "Rom-E-o."

But she continued to concentrate on raising her child well. She wanted to be the first one to see him take his first steps, to hear him say his first words, and to see him draw his first scribbles. And she wanted to love her husband, just as her mother had loved her father. This was the true reason for her existence. She, Iuccio, and the baby were a perfect union even though Iuccio rarely showed fatherly affection, for fear the child would grow up weak in character.

Iuccio's fascist know-how won him a secretarial job in the village's town hall. He resumed his political career with the arrogance of a fascist, a move that seemed to erase his mischievous past. He again frequented his old circle of friends, even if they knew that he was not as reformed as he pretended to be.

His sometimes rebellious and fractious spirit tormented his mother-in-law, who, with Herculean efforts, tried to swallow her pride and not show her anger in his presence. Nevertheless, she was worried that Angela had married beneath her station in life. This resentment toward him provoked hard feelings and grudges in both of them.

14

The monotony of village life made working there a bit hard to take. The teachers, the police, the postmaster, the midwife, the pharmacist Don Carlone, in short, all those who had come from other places in Italy, bonded with each other, becoming close friends and visiting each other frequently. The peasant proverb "Birds of a feather flock together" would aptly describe this situation.

In truth the village had nothing to offer them. There were no theaters, no cafés, no signs of social life. They were distant from the culture of the big cities that they knew, with their beautiful gardens, fountains, monuments, libraries, and museums.

The Florentine-educated Amandola, the midwife, tried to give more meaning to the daily life in the village. She became seriously interested in the unsanitary conditions since, in that period, too many children died at birth.

A woman had complained to Amandola that in this poor existence there must have been a witch who had caused the death of so many innocent children. She also claimed that the witch had been able to save some of them by pronouncing certain magic words. Naturally, Amandola did not give much weight to this story. But one day, curious, she asked the village doctor about the epidemic that affected children. Before he had a chance to answer, she saw by his facial expression that the question was a disturbingly serious one. Indeed, he verified that for the last ten years there had been a high mortality rate.

So, one beautiful September morning, while the midwife was taking a walk out of the village, enjoying the pleasant coolness of a clear blue sky, she decided to do some research. She immediately went to the town hall to examine children's death certificates, hoping to understand the reason behind the unusually high death rate.

The mayor, Domenico Magno, received her kindly into his office. He was immediately impressed by her exceptionally refined manners. Therefore, when he learned the purpose of her visit, he offered to accompany her to the only person who was familiar with such matters.

Upon seeing her, Iuccio got up from his chair, greeted her courteously, and asked her to take a seat on an old armchair. After a brief explanation, the mayor left them. She asked news about Benjamin and Angela, and he assured her that they enjoyed good health and that Benjamin was so vivacious that she would not recognize him. After this brief dialogue, Iuccio took her into a large hall where there were hundreds of booklets covered with dust.

She immediately started working and returned there often, as if she liked the odor of mold. Despite the dirtiness of the task, she was always clean and well dressed, and she wore a perfume that Iuccio found intoxicating. Winter was approaching, but when the midwife came to do her research, Iuccio, from his office, could smell only a spring perfume. He continued to look at her with a certain curiosity that soon became an unbearable passion.

15 In the meantime, a second child was born; this time Amandola, remembering the difficulties of the first delivery, was more cautious. But all went well. The baby came out head first, and as soon as he was in the hands of the midwife, he began to cry. Proudly, she asked again: "What name will you give this other beautiful boy?"

Angela turned to Iuccio, who immediately answered,

"Italo, to honor the great Italian aviator Italo Balbo." After a toast of champagne in honor of the new arrival, Amandola congratulated Iuccio, Angela, parents, and relatives and then went away.

The newborn was baptized by Giuseppe Bottai, the Fascist Party's future minister of education. Nobody in the whole province could believe that Bottai would come to a small village for such an event. Never in its thousand-year history had this parish been honored with the presence of such an illustrious political guest.

All the nobles of the village were invited to this exceptional ceremony. Amandola, the godmother, bought the bonnet and the vestment for the newborn, while Bottai, the godfather, gave Italo a silver-framed picture of the *Duce*.

After the visit from the minister of education, Iuccio's star rose to shine more brightly among the young fascists of the province. Soon he was nominated secretary of the Party. He had been born arrogant and bossy, as was the ruling regime, and he fit well into this fascist environment in which life was becoming easy and comfortable for him.

Ideologically, Iuccio was the staunchest supporter of the fascist philosophy, and Mussolini remained the only *deus ex machina*. The achievements in his political career won him new friends, while his old friends respected him much like one respects a dog for its master's sake. It was rumored that through Bottai, Iuccio also met Farinacci and Mezzasoma, Mussolini's right-hand men.

This new role put him in continuous contact with the intellectuals of the village: the physician Dr. Dei Santi; the pharmacist Don Carlone; the chief of police Don Quercia; the postmaster Don Lillo; the teachers Bichisa, Pulci and Carosella; the nurse Amandola; Don Antonio Caruso, a member of the old aristocracy; and others. He was invited to all the private parties during the winter and to all the banquets from New Year's Eve on, when snow made it impossible to leave the village.

Iuccio also started to play poker again, his childhood

pastime. Often he returned home late at night with his pockets full. Sometimes, however, he would return with his pockets empty but with the deed of this or that piece of land won from a village big shot who thought he could play better than he. But gambling did not excite him any longer. In fact, it did not matter to him anymore whether he won or lost at the card games. He was unhappy and his obsession with that lily-and-rose perfume had increased. He started courting Amandola, spending night after night pursuing her as the hunters do quails. His arrogance was equal only to that of the Fascist Party, because he was like a bulldozer, crushing any obstacle.

When he would return home in the first hours of the morning from his villainous short visits to forbidden places, his conscience would bother him because his poor innocent wife would always welcome him with an affectionate smile, an embrace and a soft kiss, caring for him tenderly, never disagreeing with him, even when she had some legitimate complaint.

"Is Angela trying to make a good husband out of me?" he would ask himself. "Is she trying to win this battle without firing a shot?"

He would have preferred an admonishment, a violent reaction on her part, just as he would have done if the case were reversed. In fact, he would have liked a real quarrel with her, just so he could disclose his secret and confess and apologize to her. By so doing, perhaps he could free himself from the disastrous situation. By talking things over with her, certainly he would be able not only to repress his bad mood, but also to operate henceforth with a serene mind, with a clear conscience. For him, confession had a healing power, after which all his sins might be washed away. It would be like breathing the clean, fresh air after a terrible storm.

The burden that he was carrying inside kept him awake at night, looking into the void of the dark with his mind in tumult. He was hoping to find some imperfection in Amandola, the siren who had bewitched him.

Despite these apprehensions, he never jeopardized his marriage, which tied him permanently to Angela and the beautiful children she had given him.

Soon after the first of the year, Eugenio Carlone, the pharmacist, a charming man, killed a pig, as was customary to do at this time of the year, and he invited his intellectual friends for a sumptuous supper. He created a pleasant environment where jokes reigned and gossiping was an art. The disposition of the seats for Eugenio's guests was a delicate matter, but he knew how to assign them, reserving the head of the table for the person of greatest respect. Therefore, it was easy even for a stranger to guess who occupied the place of honor. Iuccio seemed Christ among the apostles.

After having eaten and drunk *in vino veritas,* each tried to update the other on the latest news of the village. All the gossip came to them through servants, whom they used as panders. They were interested in everything, even the intrigues of the poor. Iuccio, who did not have servants, merely listened, knowing that the guests divulged some information in order to get his political protection for their uncertain future in the Fascist Party.

Don Antonio, for example, had been invited because he was from an old, well-established family, though he was culturally and intellectually obtuse and completely drunk. He was having great fun dispensing trivia, saying that in the village that year the birth rate of children of unknown paternity would be very high. Everyone laughed and became inquisitive and wanted to know at least who the mothers were.

He went on to relate a story that scandalized everyone present. He said that he had heard about it late one night during a warm evening in summer. Vincenzo, the shepherd, had been drinking heavily at Vedova's Tavern and told a story about the blond Genoeffe, whose husband had been working hard in America for ten years.

He said that it was toward midday on June 23, the day before Saint John's Festival, that she was returning from the river, carrying on her head the laundry that she had washed. She was sweating profusely, for the path was steep and fatiguing, winding every step for one kilometer. She stopped at Vincenzo's farmhouse, which was on the road, to ask him for some water. Since she was very tired, she also wanted to rest for a while under the shade of the two oak trees that flanked the farm like two sentinels. "Come in," said Vincenzo. "I have just returned from the well with this bucket full of fresh water. Drink as much as you want." Genoeffe, in setting down her laundry basket, unintentionally revealed her shapely bottom. Vincenzo began to shiver as if it were full winter, though he was sweating like a hog. His big muscles, like swollen plant buds in a premature spring, started to quiver. Then he took a look at her semi-exposed bosom, with that crystalline water running down that tender breast. A fresh, clean odor emanated from her body. He lost all of his senses and self-control and embraced her from behind without her being able to free herself.

"You wretch, leave me alone. You smell like a ram," protested Genoeffe.

Vincenzo ignored her. "Take off your underpanties, for God's sake!"

Genoeffe began to tremble. "I am ashamed of being in your presence."

Now, Genoeffe had been living by herself for ten years. People would sometimes talk about her being so young and beautiful, hinting that she was desirous of carnal love. But, in fact, she had always been faithful to her husband in America. Although Vincenzo wanted to enjoy her at all costs, she continued to defend herself like a young girl who did not want to lose her virginity. However, she was also made of flesh; unable to hold out against his animal strength, she finally surrendered.

Pharmacist Carlone and his guests were amazed by this story and did not know whether to believe Don Antonio, who spoke so freely. Iuccio had listened attentively, because sensational news, however trivial, was always of interest to him and the Party.

The least interested was Quercia, the chief of police, who never drank wine and who wanted to change the subject because he was totally bored. He spoke of the national progress reported in the Italian newspapers, which said that agrarian reform was at a good point. The Pontine swamps, which both Caesar and Napoleon had failed to drain, had finally been drained at a cost under the estimate, giving jobs to many people.

Iuccio added that Italian colonialism was looking toward Africa; therefore, it was important to prepare the people psychologically for a possible war against Ethiopia. According to him, it was necessary to prepare for a big propaganda campaign to induce the young people to enlist in the fascist movement. The *Duce* was waiting for a pretext, for the least provocation, for some incident along the frontier of Somalia and Eritrea to launch his campaign against Abyssinia. All listened attentively to what Iuccio had to say, especially because they knew that he was in contact with the Party's hierarchy.

It had grown late, outside, everything was under the snow. All the guests tried to arrive home, fighting against a cold wind that left the skin on their faces rough, as if they had been shaved with a dull razor.

16

Iuccio spent that night without closing an eye. The images that came to him that evening at Don Eugenio's house, indelibly imprinted in his mind, continued to bombard his brain, affected by wine. So many ideas danced in his head. He was thinking about what had been said and how the pharmacist and the doctor always gazed intently at Amandola, admiring her perfect body and her elegance, the mark of a well-to-do family, of a civility that came only from big cities. He saw in her a vigorous and ambitious woman, completely the opposite of his wife, who was perfectly content with being a housewife.

The truth was that Angela was at peace with herself and was enjoying raising her children. She taught them little songs in English, imitating a childish pronunciation as her mother had done with her. Angela knew her role well in that masculine society of fascist flags and pennants where ethics counted less than aesthetics, and where a woman counted little, resigned to the role of a fair and reserved Cinderella.

In her heart she was convinced that women, more than men, were able to resolve the big problems and sacrifices of daily life. She remembered her first experience with male chauvinism, when her history teacher took her eighth grade class on a school trip to Washington, D.C., to observe the beauties of the Capitol. From there they traveled to the State House in Annapolis, Maryland, where William Paca, an Italian-American, had been the first governor and one of the signatories of the Declaration of Independence, perhaps the greatest document in history. At the entrance to the Capitol, Paca had engraved in Italian the words *Fatti maschi, parole femmine* (Men do deeds, women talk), the state motto—words that Angela found offensive, even considering the time.

Having heard persistent rumors, Giovanni, Iuccio's best friend, hoped that Iuccio might stop pursuing an amorous relationship with Amandola. To prevent others from understanding what he was saying to Iuccio, Giovanni, being a good Latinist, said this to his friend: *"Mulier recte olet, ubi nihil olet"* ("A woman smells good when she does not use perfume").

Iuccio, however, knew that he would not have any peace until he had succeeded in conquering Amandola's heart. To distract himself from this desire, at times he would think of strange things, such as the ancient custom of the chastity belt. Such uncontrollable thought-monstrosities were not his, but those of the Devil inside of him.

While in bed he would turn and turn, breathing very lightly, almost suffocating, trying not to disturb his Mona Lisa, who was sleeping peacefully. But whenever he remembered how both the pharmacist and the physician had showered Amandola with exaggerated kindness and gentleness, he would become enraged with jealousy. The two doctors, without knowing it, were hindering his dream of getting close to this greatly admired woman. Whoever was in Iuccio's way, whoever tried to stop him—even if that person were an honest and sincere friend—would sooner or later have to pay for it.

In fact, one afternoon, while Iuccio was talking to Don Lillo, he noticed a letter in the postmaster's hands addressed to Amandola from Giuseppe Bottai, the minister of education. He would have paid anything to know its content.

Indeed, jealousy made Iuccio suspicious of everybody, friends and enemies alike. He wanted to crush them, to jail all those who competed with him socially or politically, to get them out of his way. Jealousy tortured him day and night; if he had to resort to force, he was ready. He decided to create a hostile climate, an atmosphere of distrust, sowing discord when necessary, humiliating his adversaries, and finally punishing them without any remorse, as he had been accustomed to doing whenever he felt threatened. The first step was to discredit those who stood in his way.

But discredit whom? The pharmacist? The village doctor? These men were too esteemed by the people. After thinking a while, Iuccio came up with a plan of revenge whose sole purpose was to make the unbelievable believable.

17 Iuccio was now at the pinnacle of his career, and he acted like a rooster among hens. Women were attracted to him not only for his high rank, but also for his good humor and his ability to think on his feet. He had perfected the art of mimicking, and his facial expressions easily conquered their hearts. He could be very attractive when joking and wisecracking. He flattered those whom he liked, but was known to insult those who were out of favor. He might praise a stonemason as an "engineer" or "architect," while he might call a language professor whom he disliked "the teacher of babbling tongues." If a host didn't fill his glass at a party, he would call him "the chemist who counts the drops of wine."

His political activity had given him new power. He felt strong and euphoric, and he mirrored the arrogant spirit of the Party. However, his jealousy over Amandola and his anger at being rejected by this Tuscan princess were destroying him.

To mitigate this scorching disappointment, he often reached for the bottle. On a day when he was especially intoxicated, he decided to carry out his diabolic plan. He sat down and forged the signatures of Dr. Dei Santi and the pharmacist Don Carlone, on a formal request to volunteer for military service in Eritrea. At that time the fascist government was preparing for war in Abyssinia and was accepting recruits.

Some weeks later the two unwitting volunteers received their notices to serve in the army. Rather than risk fascist retaliations, they did not contest the orders. Before departing, Dr. Dei Santi wrote the following to his family:

Dear Nephews and all of the family,
In case I do not return from this mission, you should know that I have not been the one to procure for me this Calvary. I went, knowing that Reason is meaningless against Might. A former friend planned this plot against me. In the immediate future, beware of Iuccio. I love you with the affection of a father,

Uncle Nicola

The day arrived for the two men to depart for Africa. About nine o'clock in the morning, the authorities and townspeople accompanied them out of the village with rolling drums and trumpets blasting away. Iuccio was at the head of this parade. His small eyes, reddish from lack of sleep, emitted electric shocks of glee. For such an occasion, as head of the local Party, he wore a new gray uniform with a black shirt, a hat tilted to the right, and a dagger on his side slanted toward the left part of his small body. In his shining boots, one could see reflected the movement of people.

Kindergarten children, young *Balilla* and fascists, and many other people were present to honor the two heroes of their village. At a certain point everyone stopped and the crowd became quiet. It was Iuccio's turn to praise the two volunteers who had answered the Party's call to defend the country. Many in attendance, especially the women, began to cry like children because they were about to separate from two gentlemen who served them well.

Standing like two fools, the doctor and the pharmacist could not yet believe that they were at the point of departing without their consent. The air between the two men and Iuccio was frigid. Iuccio, taking advantage of a moment of silence, started to speak:

"Comrades, young fascists, *Balilla*, sons and daughters of the She-Wolf and all other people: This is an historic hour for our small village. The sense of duty toward their country has induced two dear friends, Dr. Nicola Dei Santi and Don Eugenio Carlone, to the highest and noble sacrifice, that of serving their country. This is a great example for all of us to follow." At the end of the ceremony, all responded to the "Long live the *Duce*," and a little Fiat took the two honorees to the province's military district, from where they departed for Africa.

18

The next day, Giovanni, the usually faithful friend, went to see Iuccio to clarify certain things. Angela was so happy to see him that she immediately asked him to remain for lunch. For a few minutes Giovanni played with the children, and then, followed by Iuccio, went to the balcony where they could talk eye to eye.

"The dog never bites the master that feeds him," Giovanni began. "Those two friends that you have sent to Africa are responsible only for your rapid career. I don't understand why you are looking for trouble! You have a beautiful family and yet, with this, you risk retaliation. Do you remember the Matteotti case of 1924? Matteoti's assassination was avenged in Rome with the assassination of the fascist congressman Armando Casalini, under his daughter's eye."

Iuccio very calmly meditated for a few seconds before responding in good spirit, "Look, Giovanni, sometimes good comes out of an evil situation. Our two dear friends will serve the country well, as we all will do in order to return Italy to the old glory of imperial Rome. We will go to Africa with swords, hoes and picks, in the name of the law, to procure jobs for our workers. Until now Italy has been treated by the rest of Europe as a poor relative and it must become part of the big powers."

Indeed, Iuccio liked his role in the Party. He was sincere in his desire and belief, convinced that fascism would help people to progress and would give rise to a strong Italy. The unfair subjugation by other nations had hindered Italy from attaining greatness, but she would overcome their efforts as she had done two thousand years before.

"Iuccio, your logic is always convincing," Giovanni conceded, "and it is difficult to contradict you, but do you remember the story of the Roman statesman Menennio Agrippa that was told to the Aventinians in the fifth century B.C.? My father, who is in America, used to tell it to me in a few words, first in Italian and then in English to make his point, which was: 'One doesn't cut off his nose to spite his face.'"

"My dear friend," Iuccio replied, "it is necessary to use any means to complete our mission and to convince our young people that the ultimate sacrifice is necessary for the rosy future that the world is promised."

Their conversation was interrupted by the affectionate voice of Angela calling them to lunch. Iuccio sat at the head of the table, Giovanni to his left, Angela to the right to be nearer the kitchen, and the children, between mother and grandmother, across from Iuccio.

The guest complimented the cook and then said, "Angela, why isn't your husband a bit like you? You, with your affection, have not one enemy. You are always happy."

"It is better to have a happy heart than a full purse," she answered. "In truth, I am like my mother-in-law, who always says that love is conquered with love. Remember that love doesn't tire you."

Giovanni had grown to recognize the folly of Iuccio's plan, but held his tongue before the conversation turned into a confrontation.

Iuccio's personality invited difficult situations. He was blinded above all by his narcissism. He liked the challenge of seducing an unreachable woman like Amandola, and words were his best weapon. Yet this dalliance with the midwife would soon come to a conclusion. Bottai's letter to Amandola, which he had seen in the postmaster's hands, had made him suspicious and nervous. His doubts were confirmed one day when Iuccio learned from a friend that the prominent fascist Bottai had been struck by Amandola's seductive beauty and charming personality and that she had resisted Bottai's advances much less than his. For Iuccio this was his first defeat. He immediately gave up his diabolical plans for the beautiful midwife. From then on, he devoted himself only to his family and career.

19 The year 1935, for Iuccio, closed on a positive note. After his rapid career upwards in the fascist hierarchy, Iuccio had contributed to his Party's campaign for expansion in Africa by enlisting two dear medical friends. He had also encouraged some jobless villagers, including Termolese, Tripolino, and Pantalone, to assure bread for their families by joining the army.

He chose two of these villagers and advised them to request that they be assigned as orderlies to the two doctors. These two ruffians would keep Iuccio abreast of the activities of Dr. Dei Santi and the pharmacist Don Carlone.

As it turned out, Tripolino was sent to Eritrea and assigned to Dr. Dei Santi, who, if he had been able to choose, would have preferred the Devil as his orderly instead of this fellow townsman. The good doctor knew well that he could not trust Tripolino, having had him arrested two years before, and he remembered how difficult it had been for the police to drive him out of his cottage, like a viper out of the hole. Furthermore, Tripolino had seduced the doctor's underage maid and spent the whole night with her. "How come they sent me this crook?" asked the physician. But then, thinking and considering, Iuccio came to mind. The good doctor realized that his new orderly was a spy.

20 Mussolini's speeches continued to have positive results. The sense of "love for one's country" was felt by everybody—poor and rich, young and old, men and women, and many Italians abroad. The country was swept up in a second renaissance in which all Italians united like brothers in the pursuit of a higher cause, embraced the ideals of honesty and patriotism, and endeavored to know right from wrong, good from evil.

In this climate the *Duce* declared war on Ethiopia. Soon after his speech, all the people gathered in the square of Toro, celebrating their leader's threats to the world community, particularly to the Negus, the emperor of Ethiopia.

Anthony Mariuccia, Giovanni Don Nino, and other young fascists invaded the bell tower, ringing the bells continuously. Meanwhile, in Geneva, the League of Nations assembled to impose sanctions against Italy.

On November 19, 1935, Iuccio encouraged all the village women to follow the example of his wife, Angela, and donate their wedding rings to the war effort. They would be emulating the queen of Italy, who, the day before, had sacrificed hers. She had explained in a news article that the gold would be used to buy war materials. Iuccio clipped the entire article from the newspaper and reproduced it in big letters on a wall in the square:

Mr. President,

I would like you to know that among the many wedding rings the women of Italy offer for the glory of our great nation, there will be the king's, symbol of affection and faith, together with mine, which I offer with joy to our country. My ring represents what is dearest to me, because it reminds me of the day on which I had the fortune to become Italian.

Angela was at the head of the line and the first one to deposit her ring and her husband's in a big basket. The mayor's wife soon followed, then Mrs. Magno with her two rings, Mrs. Carlone, the pharmacist's wife, with hers, and then many more women. Finally, some prominent ladies also came, including Amandola and the teachers Bichisa, Pulci and Carosella, who brought along some gold chains.

21

Iuccio did everything to insure that his in-laws were accepting the simple country life of their village while at the same time aware of the progress and wonderful accomplishments of the fascist regime. He also wanted them to know that other nations were imitating Italian laws. For example, the eight-hour workday was a fascist concept to help people avoid becoming enslaved as they were in the past when they could not make ends meet, even by working double the eight hours. The famous document, *Carta del Lavoro* (*Charter of the Workers*), was of national interest.

Iuccio's father-in-law was not convinced. Giosué was a man of initiatives, and this controlled society suffocated him. The only one with whom Mr. Ceppone could easily communicate was Giovanni, the baker, a former American worker. He was the only one accustomed to working fifteen hours a day, ignoring the bureaucratic practices of what he considered an inept regime.

Giosué was aware that fascism had reduced criminality and that Italy was now more orderly than when he was young. But after sixteen years of America, he could not get used to an environment controlled by a few people twenty-four hours a day. He did not want to criticize the regime or compromise Iuccio's ideology. But he could see that the party-state had many faults and was lacking the democratic ways he had observed daily in America. All those demonstrations, all the assemblies, parades, and speeches that always ended with a resounding "Long live the *Duce*" seemed to Giosué a waste of time.

Giosué would ask himself: "Where are the people that I once knew, people who are responsible and capable of enormous sacrifices, people who had the courage to renew themselves every morning when they arose to fill their lungs with oxygen so that they could harvest their wheat the whole day without ever stopping or standing still? Comfort and freedom come by sweating, by working hard, and not by government-imposed rules." Nowadays, between religious holidays and fascist, patriotic Saturdays, these same people could be seen in the square responding like Pinocchio to his master, Mangiafuoco.

Assunta also was complaining to her husband. She was forced to live where she had been born, where they did not have the most essential things: running water during the whole year and heat in winter. Their disenchantment convinced them to cut the umbilical cord and go back to America, where Giosué could earn his bread and butter easily without being humiliated by anyone.

The idea of abandoning those whom they loved the most—Angela, Benjamin and Italo—pained them, but they were comforted by the fact that their daughter would be left in the good hands of Madam Nina, who had become for Angela a true mother. To avoid the usual criticism by the villagers, the Ceppones informed only the closest relatives of their plans. In the early hours of the morning, they took the train for Naples, where a ship awaited them for their return to the United States.

For Angela this was the first time that she would live

without the presence of her parents. The world did not seem the same for her any longer.

22 In May 1936, all Italians applauded the arrival of their soldiers in the Ethiopian capital. The *Duce* issued this announcement from the Venice Square balcony in Rome:

Revolutionary Black Shirts, men and women of Italy, there, beyond the mountains and the seas,

Listen. Marshal Pietro Badoglio phones: "Today, the fifth of May, at 4 P.M., at the head of the victorious troops, I have entered into Addis Ababa." During the thirty centuries of its history, Italy certainly has lived a lot of memorable times, but today is one of the most solemn.

Throughout the streets of Italy, the song "*Faccetta Nera*" ("Black Face") was sung as a symbol of the conquering Roman spirit. The *Duce* crowned King Victor Emanuel "Emperor of Ethiopia."

During the summer Dr. Dei Santi and the pharmacist Don Eugenio, returned from the victory in Ethiopia. They were welcomed by Iuccio with all the honors of heroes, as they deserved to be, having been decorated various times. The medals that they proudly displayed confirmed their heroic actions. A certificate that Dr. Dei Santi's nephews had received, stated the following: "The medical centurion, Dei Santi, having volunteered in the war of Abyssinia, has saved the life of many Black Shirts, assuming total responsibility, with his arduous medical assistance to the wounded, in front of a hostile and merciless enemy."

Among the many fascists to welcome them at the village's entrance was the hierarchy of fascist leaders, who despite the heat, wore splendid black uniforms with black boots. The mayor, the local police, and many other enthusiastic people were also in attendance.

After the usual embraces and regards, Iuccio, at the head of the parade, proceeded toward the monument of the martyrs of the First World War, where the two legionnaires deposited flowers in homage to those who had given their lives for the noblest of all causes. The entire population participated in this touching ceremony during which they continually applauded Iuccio's praises for the heroes. But the most laudatory comments could not thaw the iciness in the eyes of the two heroes, whose scrutiny, if properly directed at Iuccio, could have paralyzed him like a viper's bite. Iuccio sensed clearly that, with the return of these men, his lucky star was slowly vanishing, even though life in the Tottis' house appeared to be normal.

Dr. Dei Santi returned to public service in the same place that for many years had been home to thousands of suffering people. He was to acquire national and international fame by taking care of patients from other countries, such as the famous Israeli actress Miriam Wild. His professional and political star would ascend even more, especially after his appointment as Mussolini's personal physician. He would be able to give *Il Duce* an accurate account of Italian politics in Ethiopia, including information about industrial planning, the number of automotive shops, schools and railroads, the length in kilometers of new roads, and the status of a hospital where he had also operated. But more than anything else, the good doctor was preparing for a showdown with the man who had betrayed him. And Iuccio understood that he could not live with the sword of Damocles above his head.

After some meditation, Iuccio hung up his political gloves with pride and took the only way out that would guarantee him a future of respect, honor, a political career, and the protection of his family. He would participate in the Spanish Civil War with General Francisco Franco's fascist forces on one side and the republican bolsheviks on the other.

Without revealing his plans to anyone, Iuccio came home from his office earlier than usual one drizzly day. He embraced his wife and asked her to sit down on the sofa with him. He told her that he would have to go to Spain for a few months on a political mission, but first he would like to go on a vacation with her.

"What shall we do with our children?" she replied.

"They will be in good hands. My mother has much experience to care for them."

Angela, who lived in perfect harmony with her mother-in-law in an affectionate environment, especially after her parents' departure, agreed. Madam Nina happily acccptcd the proposal to attend to her grandchildren. She even liked the idea of Angela and Iuccio's going away for a while, because lately she had noticed they seemed sad. She wanted them to have some fun, because, with the one exception of their elopement, they had never been alone.

That same day Angela and Iuccio packed their luggage, and left the next day for Capri.

Angela found Anacapri to be a heaven on earth. Its abundance of fragrant plants and flowers intoxicated her. It had a charming ambiance. But her fascination was of short duration. She started to think about Iuccio's imminent departure to Spain. What if something went wrong for Iuccio? She quivered just thinking about it! Suddenly, as if she were going mad, she could neither see nor feel. Anxiety to return home to see her children became unbearable for her. So they cut short their stay in that paradise.

Several days later Iuccio left Toro.

23 The separation from her husband created a nightmare for Angela. Never before had she experienced such bitterness, disappointment, and pain. Only her husband's word reassured her that he was fine. He was about fifty kilometers to the south of Madrid, near Toledo, and he would soon return.

The city painted by El Greco, with its Don Quixote-like buildings, stately and proud, tall and elongated as the slender body of a matador with his sword toward the sky, seemed now bent and kneeling because of the fury and ruins of war. For the first time Iuccio came face to face with the reality of life, the tragedy of a civil war, not as battles formulated on paper during his paramilitary training. Daily he saw death head on, brothers against brothers, destruction everywhere.

In 1937, after winter had passed, Death continued to mow its path without a truce. One day, Iuccio entered a pharmacy, hoping to find some medicine to calm his stomach, which was burning like fire and causing severe pains. As in the confusion of a dream, he thought he recognized a dear childhood friend. He was right. It was Ernesto Santillo, who had come here to live and work with his pharmacist brother, Don Nicolino. Iuccio and Ernesto seemed to have been pushed together by divine power. They embraced and began to dance, jumping in the air joyfully, as they had done when they were children. They looked at each other incredulously. Here they were, far away from their village, together on foreign soil, under extraordinary circumstances.

In his excitement Iuccio asked Ernesto, "Do you remember when we were thirteen years old, promising each other that when we got married, we would help baptize each other's firstborn and become their godfathers?" Just for a moment they returned to their childhood and laughed. But then, coming back to the real world, Iuccio explained why he was in Spain, admitting that he was there for the sake of his pride, but mostly for his political survival. He was there also to defend the fascist cause and their religion against the communist anti-fascists. He was sure that that conflict would be of brief duration.

Ernesto courteously disagreed: "Dear Compare Iuccio, I am of the opposite view. This is a war that we all hate because the danger cannot be identified; no one knows who the real enemy is.

You and I could be enemies. I tell you, this bloodbath within the population makes no good sense. It has neither head nor tail. One thinks of hunting witches, of varied factions creating panic in the heart of the people. One sees thousands of innocent victims served nasty blows for breakfast and death for lunch. People are forced to dig their own graves."

For a moment Compare Ernesto was very pensive, searching for the proper words to convince Iuccio. Then he continued: "There is a very recent tragedy, that of the star that shone the most in the Spanish literary cosmos, the most popular of all the contemporary Spanish poets, Federico Garcia Lorca, who for personal and political reasons was killed and buried with three other persons: a teacher, Dioscoro Galindo Gonzales, and two anarchistic bullfighters, Joaquin Arcollas Cabezas and Francisco Galadi Melgar. They dug their own graves. The young poet, accused of crimes, but innocent like Christ on the cross, had violated no law. He had little political affiliation, and his only sin was his personal philosophy of live and let live. His human patrimony had been to recognize the dignity of all the citizens of the world. As so many other poets massacred by the fury of the anarchic violence, he had succeeded in interpreting the one feeling that people loved the most—peace. Instead, what reigned in his beloved land was pain and suffering, without love ever having a chance to blossom again. Perhaps someone had interpreted his '*Verde, que te quiero verde*' ('Green, I love you green') not as a sign of *hope* but as a sin that was serious enough to kill him."

Iuccio, for once, was speechless and got up as if he wanted to leave. He was ill prepared to debate such a question with a dear friend, under such strange circumstances, having been apart for such a long time. Ernesto also stood up but put his hand on Iuccio's shoulder. "Wait a minute. Before you go, I want to read you a poem, even if you don't understand Spanish well." Ernesto came back with a typed sheet, from which he started to read a poem of Antonio Machado, one of the best poets of his generation, on the death of his friend Federico.

45

El Crímen

Se le vió, caminando entre fuciles,
por una calle larga,
salir al campo frío,
aun con estrellas, de la madrugada.
Mataron a Federico,
cuando la luz asomaba.
El pelotón de verdugos
no osó mirarle la cara.
Todos cerraron los ojos;
rezaron: ni Dios te salva!
Muerto cayó Federico.
sangre en la frente y plomo en las entrañas.
Que fué en Granada el crimen
sabed-pobre Granada...en su Granada!

The Crime

He was seen walking between rifles,
through a long road,
walking toward the cold field,
early at the dawn, still all stars.
They killed Federico,
at the twilight of the morning.
Executioners' platoon
they didn't dare to look at his face.
All closed their eyes;
They murmured: not even God will save you!
Federico fell dead.
Blood on his face and lead in his gut.
That the crime was in Granada
you know—poor Granada...in his Granada!

They parted with a brotherly embrace, promising to see each other soon. Throughout his existence, Iuccio had learned but one truth: obedience to the Party. Now the great power of his friend's words echoed in his head.

24 Throughout 1937, the thunder of big guns intensified, as did aerial raids from both sides. For Iuccio the future was as dark as a hurricane. This was not the Africa to which he had sent his two political enemies. Uncertainty and confusion paralyzed him, making him feel like a fly in a cobweb.

He continued to think about what Compare Ernesto had told him: "In this ferocious fratricidal war there are no prisoners; brothers fight against brothers in a sea of blood. The Garibaldi Battalion, under the command of the anti-fascist Rondolfo Pacciardi, is fighting against fascist volunteers and special groups of uniformed Black Shirts in the bloody battle of Guadalajara."

Meanwhile, the stomach pains persisted. Dark thoughts felt like nails in his heart. Before falling asleep, Iuccio would be overcome with nostalgia for his family: his dear wife, his beautiful children, and finally even his mother-in-law, for whom his hatred had given way to genuine affection with a trace of humility.

An inexplicable force was urging him to return to Italy even though he realized that he would be condemned to die and his family ostracized forever. Throughout the night he would meditate on his life. Finally, he wrote a letter to his wife, asking her to call on some influential friends to intervene on his behalf. Feeling sick of the violent anarchy engulfing him, Iuccio hoped his friends might secure his transfer to Italy.

As soon as Angela received the letter, she went to Giovanni, hoping that he would resolve this matter. He, in turn, went immediately to his Uncle Angelo, who was working in Rome.

Time passed, but Iuccio did not receive the news he

expected. The correspondence between the couple intensified. Iuccio reacted with heightened anxiety and then panic when Mussolini initiated his racist policy against the Jews, causing an exodus from the old continent toward the new and reinforcing Iuccio's doubts about the fascist ideology.

The American embassy in Rome advised its citizens to leave Italy immediately. Angela received a letter from the embassy, requiring her to repatriate or risk losing her citizenship. Her course of action was clear. She could depart without her family, but as soon as she arrived in America, she could apply for her family to come.

Immediately she informed Iuccio, who lost no time in asking his childhood friend, Ernesto, to send a letter in his behalf. A letter coming from Ernesto would be less likely to be intercepted by the fascist secret police. In the letter Iuccio begged his wife to try to accelerate his application for transfer. He also told her not to worry about their children, because, with Giovanni's help, he would be enrolling them for the time being in the Convitto Nazionale, a private school in a nearby town where Francesco, one of their cousins, was studying.

Angela trusted only Giovanni in these matters. She urged him once more to ask his Uncle Angelo to expedite Iuccio's transfer and their own departure. Not too long after, Angela received authorization from the American consulate to leave the country. There was no trace of Iuccio's request.

The idea of returning to her native land with her family had been a dream she had secretly nurtured for a long time, but she had never dared to reveal it to anyone so as not to jeopardize her husband's political ambitions. That desire weighed too much on her conscience. Now that she was forced to abandon her family, her world collapsed. Everything seemed difficult, and she was scared.

And yet, the ever-faithful Angela deferred to her husband's wishes and proceeded with the help of her family to fix the date for her departure as soon as possible. As arranged, Giovanni took care of the children's schooling by putting them in the private school where they would join their cousin Francesco. The time to separate from her children arrived, and what prevented her from going crazy was the idea that in a short time they would be reunited in the land of the free. She embraced her children, and nobody was able to separate them.

The kitchen that until a little while ago had been full of joy and warmth was now full of sadness and tears. The alarm clock on the fireplace ticked loudly as if to remind her that these were the last minutes together for the three pounding hearts beating loudly as one. The carriage was waiting outside for her children to be taken away to the private school. Exhausted and numb, she let herself be separated from the children. Shc fclt like a flower budding early in March, killed by a sudden freeze.

As soon as the children were in the coach, Bianchino whipped the horses. That smack augmented her sorrow. She fixed her eyes on the two little faces that were looking back at her, not able to cry any longer. In their eyes she saw their hearts, and then the coach was gone.

A little later Angela, too, departed. Some relatives accompanied her to the train that took her to Naples, where she embarked on the ship the *Saturnia*, setting sail a while later.

25 As soon as she arrived in America, Angela went to live with her parents. Immediately she telephoned her father-in-law, who lived in Piedmont, West Virginia. "Hello, who is this?"

"Hello, Dad. It's me—Angela. How are you? I bring you the affectionate regards of everybody, and I want to assure you that everybody is well, even Iuccio in Spain."

"Spain? What is he doing in Spain?"

"It's a long story, and I will tell you as soon as I see you. My wish is to see you as soon as possible."

"You will be the most beautiful gift that Santa could bring me this year."

"Then will you come for Christmas? You can stay with us as long as you want."

Grandfather Benjamin did indeed arrive on Christmas Eve with two valises full of gifts. There were gifts for Angela, Assunta, and Giosué, and gifts for his loved ones still in Italy— Madam Nina, Iuccio, the small Italo, young Benjamin—in hopes that soon the whole family would arrive from Italy and be finally reunited.

Blood in Angela's veins had not been circulating since the day she had been forced to separate from her children. But because of the holidays, she did not want to cause any grief so she put on a good front for her father-in-law and her parents, hiding well her true feelings. She, too, put gifts under the Christmas tree. The stay at the Ceppones' was a beautiful experience, above any expectation for Iuccio's father, who was used to many years of solitude. After a week's stay, he returned home unwillingly, happy that his son had married a lovely and kind girl. However, he regretted that his son had blindly embraced the fascist ideology, defending it in the massacre that came from the civil war in Spain.

Soon after her arrival, Angela, with her parents, traveled to the Italian consulate in Cleveland, Ohio, to apply for her family to come to America. The chancellor explained that, according to the law, Angela would have to wait for three months before she could apply. Her pleas for an exception were in vain.

Stunned by the ruling, the three left the building and returned to the train station. Angela sobbed all the way. The bitter air coming from Lake Erie to the west of the city froze her tears. Her mother begged her to stop crying, because people, oblivious to the foul weather, were staring at the unusual spectacle of a beautiful woman sobbing.

From that day on, Angela found comfort in going to church, abstaining from food, and sending money to the poor. Desperate, she turned directly to God with her pure heart. She missed her family desperately, especially her children, and she prayed that they be saved in the event of a war.

26

In 1939 the Italian troops in Spain took the city of Barcelona from the communists. The powerful anti-fascists, from Nenni to Togliatti, lost their ideological struggle to advance their cause. With fascist and Nazi help, General Francisco Franco emerged as the *caudillo*, dictator of the Spanish people, putting an end to the deadly conflict that had taken the lives of 4,658 Italians and wounded 10,897. Mussolini declared victory over the communists in Spain.

Iuccio finally returned home, but in spite of the fascist victory, he found that he himself had lost. The fears, the suffering were all in vain. He discovered that Dr. Dei Santi's nephew now occupied his old position at the city hall and had no intention of leaving it. The new assignment the Party gave Iuccio amounted to taking documents from one office to the other, which hardly seemed a promotion for a war veteran. He clearly understood that after three years of absence, the cat had lost and the mice had won. He asked whether he could be transferred to the nearby capital of the region, where he could also provide a better education for his children.

One day he received the letter from Angela for which he had been waiting so anxiously. His eyes jumped over the opening lines, quickly looking for the part that would talk about the application that would take him and his children to America. But he could not find it. He reread the letter word for word without finding that important news.

For an instant his heart stopped functioning, then began to beat strongly as if it were looking for a way out of his body. He reread the letter once more, but the message was the same: "It is necessary to still have patience for some months before we can apply for your visa." He started to sweat profusely. Choked by this bad news, he had to sit down to reflect on his next step.

After a month of suffering in the village, frustrated by an

odious job and by an uncertain future, Iuccio finally got the position in Campobasso for which he had applied. There he found a small room in a boardinghouse on Garibaldi Street next to the Convitto Mario Pagano, the private boarding school in which he had enrolled his children. The boardinghouse was such a pleasant environment that after a few months he brought his children to live there with him.

The Albanos, the host family, consisted of five people in a household that worked like a clock. There was Mrs. Albano, the mother, who was an expert in culinary matters and occupied herself mostly with the kitchen. There was her thirty-six-year-old daughter, Ersilia, a solitary woman and already a *zitellona* or old maid who tended to Iuccio's personal care, such as ironing his shirts and pants, and even taking fresh coffee to his room in the morning; nineteen-year-old Rita, who devoted herself to washing and ironing clothes; and Marilena, a student in the middle school, who cleaned the house. One other daughter was forty years old and married, and lived in Rome.

The boys, Benjamin and Italo, were happy. Even though the house was small, they were treated as if they were part of the family. The atmosphere here was affectionate, not at all severe, and therefore markedly different from that of the private school, where at eight o'clock at night they had to turn off their lights and not stir until the next morning. But, despite the warmth of their new surroundings, the children, in their hearts, felt their mother's absence, and nobody could lessen their loneliness. They would not accept Ersilia as a kind of stepmother, no matter how affectionate she tried to be. Before their arrival, Ersilia had lost the enthusiasm to live because every dream she had had to have a family had faded away. But now, with the advent of these unexpected tenants, she had regained the smile and the peace that cruel destiny had denied her. The whole family noticed her new good humor in her approach to life.

27 In March 1939, the German war machine advanced inexorably, conquering what remained of Czechoslovakia. Iuccio had not yet received news concerning his visa for America. Two months later Mussolini signed the famous Steel Pact with Hitler, provoking in Iuccio continuous worries and fears that these new events could hinder his reunion with his wife. There was so much to be done before the papers would arrive authorizing their departure. For example, it was necessary for the three of them to have a blood test, a procedure that required much time.

The Second World War began on September 1. Even though Italy was for the moment neutral, communications were suspended. There were no doubts the Totti family had been divided, but now it appeared the separation might last a long time. Their fears were confirmed in June of 1940, when Mussolini allied himself with Hitler, despite the unpopularity of the war with the majority of Italians, who responded with little enthusiasm to his pronouncement:

> Fighters of the earth, of the sea and of the air, Revolutionary Black Shirts, Men and women of Italy:
>
> The hour marked by our destiny has struck. We go out into the field of Evil, against the plutocratic reactionary democracies of the West, which have hindered our march every time in the past and even laid a trap for the very existence of the Italian people. The declaration of war has been given to the ambassadors of Great Britain and France, June 10, 1940.

In the meantime, the graduating class of 1940 had been called to bear arms. Among them was Giovanni. Iuccio accompanied him to the train station, reassuring him that everything would go well because the war would not last long. In reality his hope for a final, not too distant victory had been shattered.

"Not all evil things result in harm," Giovanni told him.

"What do you mean?"

"For the love that I have for you and your children I hope that you will be exempted from serving in the army because you have two children without their mother."

"Giovanni, I hope so—for their sake," Iuccio replied, embracing him. A few minutes later they heard a long, thin whistle from the conductor, announcing the train's departure. Many people were crying. Iuccio was biting his lips, trying to restrain his emotions.

Day after day war bulletins brought encouraging news, describing victories on land and sea, and in the air. The Rome-Berlin-Tokyo Axis seemed to be invincible. Only rarely would the media mention losses, such as those in East Africa, Greece, and Russia.

Iuccio had lost the patriotic spirit that once would have brought him to martyrdom for his fascist cause. His sadness over the separation from his wife supplanted the pride that he once had in his country. He remembered only an antagonizing motto of Mussolini: "How is it possible, in a country of servants, not to become a master?"

He was not going to be deceived anymore about the final outcome of the war. He was holding fast to the truth. He would trust only what his eyes saw and his ears heard. There was a cavalry training center under the building in which he lived, and every day he saw soldiers training for horseback riding. At the same time he read in the newspapers that the German war machine was crossing the European continent.

It was obvious to him that Mussolini had won the first game in Ethiopia and the second in Spain against the communists, and that now he was gambling on the third, fighting with means that were ineffective or at best like those of World War I. It seemed that this game would be lost.

Then he heard people talking about hunger brought on by a 200-gram-a-day ration of bread that often contained sawdust. This is what his eyes saw and his ears heard. For him, this was the truth of the matter.

28 Benjamin, being a model son, did not mind sleeping in his father's room. He was always obedient, and at school he listened attentively to the teachers, getting the highest grades in his class, just as his mother had done at his age. His uncle, Monsignor Nicola Totti, knowing Benjamin's virtues, had often expressed his desire to bring the boy to Penne, a city in the region of Abruzzo, where he would have been able to send him to a school of the prelate's liking. Though the boy would be under the watchful eye of a well-to-do religious uncle, Iuccio had refused.

Italo, as the younger of the two, was also the more sensitive, but he was happy to sleep in the same room with Rita and Marilena, the Albano daughters.

During the winter the two girls let him sleep between them to protect him from the cold weather, cuddling him and kissing him as if he were a doll. But he wanted only his mother's warmth, finding it very hard to break from his mother's umbilical cord. The lack of motherly love made him restless. In fact, in school the teachers would complain of his mischievousness. He was so uneasy and rebellious that they had to use a stick in order to calm him down.

The teachers recommended two tutors to address Italo's lack of achievement: Carlo Levi, teacher of mathematics, and David Contino, teacher of Italian, Latin and Greek—both politically confined Jews who were famous in Campobasso for their ability not only as teachers but also as good psychologists. However, neither the tutors nor Iuccio realized that it was Italo's mischievousness that made him forget temporarily the painful separation from his mother when she left for America.

The two tutors were well aware of Iuccio and his political past. After arranging the price and the time for the lessons, Professor Levi addressed Iuccio: "Dear Mr. Totti, before you go away, we want to clarify the matter of our Italianism. We Jews have been in Italy since Caesar's time, before Christ; and among the one hundred kilometers of catacombs, there is also a Jewish one on Torlonia Street in Rome, a symbol of our long presence and a source of energy for us. It is where our roots are. We are as Italian as you are. Our history is yours. What the Romans did to the Etruscans, you have done and continue to do to us. What remains of the Etruscans are only the cemeteries, while we still have our ghettos." He wanted to continue, but Iuccio, bewildered, stopped him, saying that he was no longer the man he was in the past and that he was able to walk in their shoes, because he too had been persecuted by destiny. They shook hands like friends and Iuccio departed.

Often after school, Italo would stay to play with and challenge other students, a routine that led to mischievousness. His secret was the element of surprise, hitting first with a meter stick but using it as a sword, as if he were one of the Three Musketeers. He could act with bravado knowing that he could count on the intervention of his cousin Francesco, who was in the same school, but a lot bigger than Italo's opponents and whose big peasant shoes were enough to frighten them all away.

One day Italo was playing with some companions around an old threshing machine behind his house when he put his right hand in the shredder. Italo lost part of his thumb, and the whole index and middle fingers. He was taken immediately to the nearby Cardarelli Hospital, some hundred meters away. Madam Nina, Iuccio's mother, weak as she was, upon hearing the bad news, suffered a heart attack and died.

Because of these tragedies, Iuccio became so numb that whenever anyone spoke to him at the house or at the office, he would not answer. His fountain of jokes that had made him so popular was now dry. For a long time he wore a black band on his arm as a sign of mourning, and he often went to the cemetery, seeking solace. He had never revealed his love for his mother, a love that had been his Achilles' heel.

29 At that time the government had put posters on the walls throughout the city, telling people to paint their window panes, a measure that would keep the city in the dark and deter aerial raids. The militia, worrying about plots and uprisings, had placed itself at strategic checkpoints to monitor people entering and leaving the city.

The government's food rations were insufficient, especially for people like Iuccio, who had two young mouths to feed. Iuccio contacted Aunt Maria Salvato, a farmer, whose husband had emigrated to America. He proposed to provide assistance for her son Francesco's schooling and intellectual development in exchange for bread for his children. She remembered her husband's words when he wrote to her from America: "Dear Maria, I ask you, for the love that ties us, to enroll our Francesco into a sound educational system at all costs."

Aunt Maria was an illiterate farmer, but she recognized the great need for her son's education and therefore committed herself to great acts of self-denial. Once or twice a week, early in the morning, she would go to Campobasso with a basket on her head, filled with foodstuff such as oil, beans, potatoes, bread, and wine. She often crossed muddy terrain to avoid the militia at their checkpoints, arriving exhausted at the Albanos', Francesco's new domicile.

For this and other reasons, Francesco strived to be a perfect son, never wanting to disappoint his mother, and respecting relatives and people in general. He even began calling Iuccio "Uncle" as a sign of respect, obeying him as if he were a true nephew.

30 Some months after his mother's death, while Iuccio was at work in his office, a lady came in for a certificate. Her similarity to Angela sent shock waves through his body, momentarily stunning him. The whole day he did nothing else but think about his wife.

When he returned to the Albanos' that evening, he ordered Francesco to buy a gallon of red wine. It did not take him long to become drunk. Marilena did not like his behavior toward Francesco, who was too nice to be treated like a servant. More than once she had thought of confronting Iuccio to reveal her indignation. This time she did, even though he was inebriated. But all her reproaches that evening were in vain because the day after, Don Iuccio, as they were now accustomed to calling him, did not remember anything about what had happened the night before.

Meanwhile, Benjamin was away studying at a school of the Salesian religious order at Torre Annunziata near Pompeii. As soon as schools closed for Christmas vacation at the end of 1942, Iuccio asked Francesco to take a small package to Benjamin for the holiday, an errand he accepted with enthusiasm. Iuccio had convinced Aunt Maria that the trip would be a good educational experience for her fourteen-year old son, to see the world as it really is. And so on a beautiful morning Francesco left.

The overloaded bus on which Francesco was traveling was going slowly as if something was going to happen. Actually, when it arrived in Benevento, it broke down. The driver announced that it would take a good hour before it could be fixed.

One of the young people who had been traveling on the bus motioned to the others to follow him, telling them that he knew a place where they could spend some time. Francesco obediently followed them, step by step, because he was a minor. Upon arriving at the front door of the designated place, they all stood in line to enter. Francesco succeeded in walking right in, taking advantage of the chaos created by the last man, who, not having an ID card, forced himself in. Soon a corpulent woman approached Francesco, who followed her into a little room.

"ID, please," the woman demanded.

"They took it from me at the door."

"Do you have money?"

"Enough." And he emptied his two pockets on a table.

She looked at him with a kind smile and asked, "Why are your legs shaking?"

"I am in a hurry. I have to take the bus waiting for me outside for Torre Annunziata."

"Then, hurry up. Take off your pants and underwear."

She had hardly touched him when she felt sprinkled as if by a hose. He understood for the first time what he had not learned during the catechism or while studying Dante. How beautiful heaven really was!

He arrived back at his village on Christmas Eve, the envy of his friends for being, like Marco Polo, a veteran of a long trip. Little did they know!

31 In January 1943, schools reopened later than usual because of a lack of fuel and an unusual snowfall. One night after supper, Marilena and Francesco were alone in the small living room doing their homework together. Around a brazier a blanket hung over their knees to trap the heat emanating from the charcoal, as it had warmed them so many other times.

Marilena was becoming very attached to Francesco. "I really want to help you to learn Latin, Greek, history, geography, and mathematics; but first I have to remove from my mind something that has been bothering me for a long time." She hesitated for a moment before asking, "Why are you afraid of your Uncle Iuccio, who is really not your uncle because he married your Cousin Angela?"

Francesco had known her for some time, and he cherished her continual gentleness and concern, but above all he liked her natural beauty and charms as well as her sense of justice. He answered calmly, with the maturity of an older man. "You are right. So many people don't understand my relationship with him. Really, I don't understand it myself. I can only tell you that once bitten by a snake, you are afraid of a lizard. I always hear my mother's voice telling me, 'Be good to everybody, because you don't have a father, as the others do.'"

With a kind look Marilena encouraged him to continue.

"My mother wants me to be like the universe—perfect. When my father left for America, she entrusted me to my good brother-in-law, Saverio, a very straight person who is respected by everybody. He wanted to keep his promise to his mother-in-law, but at times he was too strict with me, even using force when necessary to keep me from doing anything wrong."

With that same sweet smile she led him to continue.

"I remember one spring afternoon during the Easter vacation. I was eight years old and in the third grade. My brother-in-law asked me to take some lambs to graze down in the valley, near a brook where the grass was fresh and tender. I started looking at these little animals; and the more I looked at them, the more I wanted to protect them at all costs from going to a slaughterhouse. I saw in their eyes that eternal peace that I loved so much, and the thought of their being killed before Easter tormented me. Unconsciously, I suppose, I made it my mission to try to save them, knowing that they were going to be slaughtered.

"To divert my attention, I lay down on the velvety grass, looking at the blue sky above me. The weather was so pleasant and mild, with the sun warming me as the brazier does us now. The divine music of nature was relaxing and I fell asleep. In my dream I saw Saint Francis of Assisi, patron saint of animals, who told me that he would have protected those innocent lambs. When I woke up, I looked everywhere, but I couldn't find those little animals. Crying and not knowing what to do, I raced back to my brother-in-law to explain what had happened. That Holy Week became a hell for me after the nasty beating Saverio gave me for losing the lambs. Since then, I have always obeyed. Those blows did to my mind what hunger does to the body. But I have to admit that, in one way or another, they shaped me."

Marilena was so touched by that cruel story that she told him, "You have a great heart and in it I see part of myself." Then she embraced him with a prolonged kiss. Francesco for the first time felt like a hero, as if he had conquered Mount Everest; and for a moment his body seemed to be energized by the electricity in that little room in Benevento. But then he realized that this sensation was different as the two looked at each other tenderly.

Their eyes met again, arousing overpowering affection. As they were drawn to each other, they were interrupted by her mother's call.

"Marilena!"

"Yes, Mother!"

"It is ten o'clock and tomorrow it is a school day."

"I am coming. I will put the blanket away and bring the brazier immediately."

As he left to go to his room, Francesco was licking his lips as if she had left honey there. In reality it was only her lipstick.

32

It was Mardi Gras, 1943, the middle of a mad war in which traditions no longer were part of life. Iuccio received a letter of condolence from Giovanni for his mother's death:

River Don, December 18, 1942

Dear Iuccio,

Only I know how much you loved your mother, even though you never showed it. Her death must have caused endless grief....

We are camped here near the River Don with our comrade German soldiers, spending day after day in the company of our brothers, that is, wind, snow and cold. We are learning well the art of living in a tragedy—how to survive without provisions in a dangerous situation. As you know, I belong to the Swift division, which, together with the Tridentina, Julia, Cuneense, Cosseria, Ravenna, Turin and Sforzesca, is here at the disposition of the German High Command.

Among so many bitter episodes I want to tell you one that overwhelms all the negative ones. I met a girl named Nastasia, who had hidden herself in a stable during a search, and I fell immensely in love with her. Since then, I have protected her and promised to marry her as soon as possible. She is carrying my child, my future descendant, who, if he or she resembles her, will be the most beautiful star in this universe.

Affectionately, Giovanni

It was the last letter Giovanni wrote, because he and his comrades were forced into a cursed withdrawal that later became "the march of death." Nobody ever knew where, when or how Giovanni, our little hero, lost his life, nor did anyone ever learn the fate of Nastasia and her child.

33 For Benjamin, Iuccio had chosen well the Salesian private school at Torre Annunziata near Naples. He did not want his son to take the same tortuous road that he had traveled. But the more time passed, the more he worried about the bombardments in the big cities.

When Iuccio heard about the raid on the railway station in Naples, he immediately thought of taking his son out of the Salesian school, which was close to that big city. The explosion was so big that it seemed as if another Vesuvius had been born a few kilometers from the true one. Iuccio did not hesitate to telephone the director of the institute to tell him that he would be sending a messenger by taxi to bring Benjamin back. While at the table that evening, Iuccio kindly asked Francesco to get ready early in the morning to deliver his son's letter of release from the Salesian Institute at Torra Annunziata. In the closet there would be a new pair of shoes for him to wear so that he would appear properly dressed when he introduced himself to the Salesian Fathers.

After supper, Marilena and Francesco went to the small

living room and sat near the warm brazier to do their homework as they had done so many times before. As soon as they were alone, Marilena told him, "I have a gift for you—a new pair of shoes."

Francesco smiled and shook his head. "I appreciate your concern, but I could never accept your offer, because I could not betray my mother's frugal spirit. It was she who, in 1941, asked Master Peppe, the expert shoemaker, to make for me shoes large enough to last the whole war. Besides, Iuccio has already provided a pair."

"But sooner or later, you will need new shoes."

"Marilena, I understand the shame that I am bringing on all of you, but soon I will also resolve this problem. I am at the right age and soon the moment will come for me to enroll in the M Battalions. Then you will see me dressed up anew like a hawthorn in spring, and you will be proud of me."

"What are the M Battalions?"

"They are for underage youths, who at sixteen years of age can enlist to go to war. The 'M' stands for Mussolini."

That story touched her soul. She embraced him with a long kiss on his lips, where she again left only the sweet taste of honey.

The next day Francesco left for Torre Annunziata, returning at night with Benjamin. As soon as the boy saw his father, he wanted to jump in his lap so great was his joy at being together again, away from the bombardments. They embraced, and then he kissed his brother and all the others.

Iuccio left his office a little earlier the next afternoon, eager to play with his son before it got dark, but he also had some important news to discuss with him. There had been very little communication between father and son until then. Communicating with others might have been Iuccio's forte, but it was not so with his own children.

As soon as he arrived home, he went out on the balcony where he could watch Benjamin playing in the garden with the chickens. Although he had an urgent matter to discuss, he did not want to disturb Benjamin while he was having so much fun, laughing at the poor chickens who for some reason were falling down one after the other.

When he went down to investigate, Iuccio found a small frying pan with some wine in it. The chickens were intoxicated! At first he wanted to scold his son, but then he started laughing himself, happy to see some good humor in Benjamin, who until then seemed a solemn child. Iuccio was reassured that there was some mischievousness in Benjamin, a quality that, in his eyes, made the boy normal.

Iuccio wanted to speak to Benjamin about the war and its vicissitudes. He had decided that his son would go to live with his uncle in Penne, a safer place to be, away from the bombardments, where he would finish his education.

Benjamin was obedient as always. A week later, accompanied by Francesco, he took the train to Pescara, and from there went on to his uncle's town. Now Iuccio had only to worry about his younger child, whom he had to watch twenty-four hours a day because Italo had abundant energy and was full of mischief. Francesco also felt good about the role he had played in getting Benjamin to a safer place.

34 In 1943 bombs struck everywhere. Reports of these raids contradicted the euphoric news on the radio. The Allies, welcomed as liberators, disembarked in Sicily with few casualties. The national situation worsened on July 25, when fascism fell. It was humiliating and painful for young fascists to see the disintegration of the Fascist Party.

The morning of July 26, the mayor of Francesco's village was spotted in a white shirt and a red tie as he headed toward city hall. One could hardly recognize in this subdued little man the energetic fascist who had proudly worn a black shirt just a few days ago.

"Yesterday black, today red and white. One of these days I will spit in the face of that double-faced wretch," commented Giovanni Termolese, one of those who had volunteered to fight in Africa.

The rumor was circulating that in Naples the sudden fall of fascism had also caught the Germans by surprise. They were going through the streets with white handkerchiefs on their arms, in a show of their pacific intentions.

Between the Allied bombardments and the Germans' last-ditch defense, nobody knew what to do or which road to take to safety. On August 19, 1943, the Basilica of St. Lawrence in Rome suffered a direct hit. On August 29 the main aqueduct in Naples was shelled, leaving the city without water. On September 1, after a bombardment of Ortona, near Pescara, Iuccio tried in vain to communicate with his son in Penne. For Benjamin it was too dangerous to go back to Campobasso now, considering that the Germans were retreating on the highway, the National Adriatic, toward Pescara, which was of some strategic importance to them. After the first forty-five days of chaos, from July 25 to September 8, 1943, General Badoglio announced, "The war continues."

Soon every means of communication, by land or sea, was interrupted. What many people were quietly thinking was indeed happening. The Italians were becoming prisoners in their own homes.

Soldiers, ragged, dusty and barefooted, were scattering throughout the peninsula, terrified of being taken prisoner by the Germans.

Francesco's brother-in-law, Saverio, escaped the Greek front mostly on foot but sometimes by train, crossing through Yugoslavia and northern and central Italy. When Francesco met him in Campobasso for the first time in four years, Saverio looked like Ulysses returning to Ithaca.

Like so many other footloose soldiers after September 8, Natangelo Paulino, one of the very few who volunteered to join the M battalions, succeeded in escaping from Turin. He arrived in

Toro, Francesco's village, with a brand new military truck that looked like a freshly minted coin. The young soldier did not waste any time dismantling the truck, hiding all its parts in different places around the village. Then he, like the others, went to hide in the hills.

35 The Germans had taken possession of some houses near Francesco's. Like spiders, they paralyzed the citizenry in their web so that now the unfortunate villagers were trapped, forced to observe the events that passed under their eyes but helpless to do anything. As children need their security blanket, the Germans clutched their machine guns. Villagers were living a nightmare and life was unbearable. People did not speak to each other in the streets. It was as if they were anticipating a cataclysm that would swallow them sooner or later.

The Germans established a curfew, from seven in the evening to seven in the morning. On the first night of the curfew, with police help, the new masters gathered thirty twelve- to fifteen-year-old boys who had violated the curfew. Nobody knew whether these boys were ignorant of the new manifesto, or whether they simply wanted to defy their unwanted guests. Francesco was among the group but escaped.

The new laws were clear. No one could leave his home after the authorized time without authorization—not even priests, monks, or nuns. Only the village doctor was free to circulate.

Some farmers, led by Francesco's mother, Maria Salvato, complained to the mayor that they could not properly tend their animals during the designated hours. They presented him with a list of one hundred protesters, all in alphabetical order.

The despotic mayor, who had never allowed the people to discuss an issue, now showed his human side for the first time, assuring them that he would discuss the matter with the police. The police chief, who during the war had been Public Enemy

Number One, also welcomed the farmers' petition. Moved by compassion and feeling like a philanthropist, he was ready to help his people. Immediately he went to see Captain Hans Pupp, the German commander, whose headquarters were in a modest house in the square from where he could easily observe the comings and goings of the people.

The captain looked at the list of the farmers and, without hesitation, called his secretary and dictated a modification of the curfew that would exempt all farmers from the original order. The chief of police was surprised by the sudden decision, and his sixth sense suggested that something wasn't quite right.

The following day, after the new manifestos were posted, a villager proudly announced, "They wanted to put the muzzle on us as if we were dogs, but we showed them. It is necessary to show your teeth to get some respect." The villagers did not yet realize that the German captain had bamboozled them all with one stroke of genius, for, with that list, Captain Pupp had found an easy, legal way to get the daily provisions of rabbits, turkeys, lambs, cows, and everything else that he needed.

Sometime later, the Germans found the skeleton of the truck hidden by Natangelo Paulino. In this case, however, the Germans were determined to show their severity if their orders were not followed. In the square they put up a manifesto that began, "*Der Deutsche Kommandant*," and went on to warn that if the truck were not reassembled within forty-eight hours and ready to be used, many citizens would be shot. This was an almost impossible mission. Fortunately, a group of courageous people succeeded in finding Natangelo hiding in the hills. He was able to reassemble the precious truck and deliver it to the Germans within the time limit, thus avoiding a slaughter.

That same afternoon, Francesco, who was still in Campobasso, said goodbye to Iuccio, Marilena and all the others, left the city on foot, and hurried toward his village. It took him thirty-five minutes to run ten kilometers. He was concerned about his mother's living alone. When he arrived all sweaty, he found three Germans and an unknown militiaman searching his house, hoping to find wheat, corn or any foodstuff for their survival. Maria's name was on that infamous list of one hundred farmers who had protested the curfew. After a thorough search, the Germans found only one ham, and left. Fainting from fear, his mother fell onto the pavement like a ripe pear from a tree.

Francesco had participated in all the fascist organizations from the She-Wolf, the smallest fascist pioneers, to *Balilla*, and then Young Fascist, and had even thought about enlisting in the M Battalions. Now he felt betrayed by fascism and imprisoned by the former ally. He went to his bedroom and erased these words written on the wall behind the bed:

> BENITO MUSSOLINI
> Leader of Italy
> His love for Italy
> Which he wanted great
> Free and respected
> Fought against hate
> Of predominant powers
> Who wanted our nation
> Weak, derided and enslaved
> Betrayed by perverts
> Sold to the foreigners
> By scurvy who did not know
> The sense of duty
> Deprived of honor
> Killed by him who feared
> The inexorable justice
> Wanted to continue
> To ensure
> Personal liberty
> Sacrificing everything
> To free motherland

For some twenty months, Italy became a battleground that shifted slowly from the south northward. To die young was considered somewhat of a blessing, an honorable escape from an uncertain future. Italy was drowning in the blood from daily slaughter. A civil war seemed imminent, and only the rogues would survive the violence.

These were sorrowful days of nervousness and insomnia. Rumors spread that the Germans were gathering up young people in their war effort, and nobody was allowed to circulate without an ID card. Many villagers avoided the German patrols by going into hiding in the hills and in caverns. In the big cities ex-soldiers, ex-fascists, Jews, socialists and anarchists, without distinction, were sheltered in churches where they passed the time playing cards elbow to elbow, in full harmony.

Many young and elderly people were captured and put on northbound trains. Mercurio Ferrara and Americo Fascia were taken prisoners by the Germans, but luckily they succeeded in getting off the trains on their way to Austria, after the partisans sabotaged them. They described three days of absolute horror. The news had a terrifying effect on people, provoking an immediate psychosis that sent them running away like frightened rabbits. The only people who circulated through the village were the very old, on whose faces one could see the signs of terror. Of the 716,000 Italian soldiers interned by the Germans after September 17, 1943, the repatriated survivors of war numbered around 550,000. The others died in various prisoners' camps.

36 In the last week of German occupation, Iuccio met the two Jewish teachers, Levi and Contino, who had been confined in Campobasso for political reasons. They had come to city hall to sign in as they had done routinely morning and evening, as all the political dissidents were required to do by the fascist authority. By now, Iuccio, so greatly devastated by recent events, disliked the Fascist Party and felt a certain brotherhood with the two teachers.

He also had felt a certain obligation toward them because

they had resolved his son's scholastic problems. He told them that he would stop by after supper for a brief visit. He wanted to express his gratitude for what they had done for Italo. That was only an excuse because these were days of distrust and vengeance. His real motive was to propose a plan that could save them from the Germans. Iuccio knew a monsignor in the city of Campobasso, a close friend of his uncle, Monsignor Totti.

When Iuccio left them, the two were skeptical. After all, Iuccio was an old fascist. Was this a trick so that he could get favors from the Germans? Or was Iuccio thinking that the two Jews could be witnesses in his favor after the liberation? In the past, the two Jews had never trusted him, because they had been watched by Iuccio himself. They remembered the time when they went to the mayor's office to sign in and Iuccio had screamed at them. But ultimately they accepted his plan.

Much of the time one could hear and see waves of Allied airplanes coming from the south, flying north where they continually unloaded tons of bombs. In the meantime the Allies continued to hammer the village of Toro. The Canadians' guns were a few kilometers away and had already struck some people in the valleys. It looked like fireworks during a holiday, and the 120-millimeter shells produced a particular roaring sound announcing their arrival. And on the village's outskirts one could feel the invisible presence of the Allies.

From his farm Francesco saw some bombs exploding near his house in the southern part of the village, where the Canadian artillery was aiming. Later he learned that a shell had exploded in front of a house on The Old Street, under the police station, the intended target. The house belonged to a thirty-six-year-old woman named Maria Teresa Grossa who, upon hearing the first booms of artillery, had looked out the window facing the southern part of the valley and the Tappino River. She had just called to her children, who were tending the sheep grazing not too far away, when the shell exploded. It was a direct hit. Mariangela, her seven-year-old daughter, died instantly. Maria Teresa, who was several months pregnant, was wounded in the head by a piece of shrapnel and died twelve hours later.

Cruel destiny also prevented Amandola from realizing her mission of taking care of the wounded and sick. While she was assisting some wounded in a shelter, she herself was wounded. A fragment of shrapnel entered her heart, and she died a few minutes later, to the horror of those around her. The bad news spread with lightning speed. Despite the immediate danger from Allied bombs and fierce German soldiers, everyone participated the next day in Amandola's funeral.

After some weeks of attack and counterattack, the Germans decided to leave the village. As if to demonstrate that their departure was of their choosing and that they were not scared, two Germans made a point of going to the shoemaker, Master Nicola, whose shop was near the square, and asking him to fix their shoes. While one was with the cobbler, the other was a few meters away, looking around and standing guard. Outside, their motorbike with its sidecar was running, ready to leave at the first sign of trouble.

The Germans' arrival in the square two months earlier had been far different. The Germans had made so much noise that the windows began rattling. Bewildered people watched the river of German machines; the children cheered them on. Of all the vehicles, the ones that impressed the most were the armed tanks. One, which was baptized Tiger, took up residence in the square; the other, Panther, had been parked under a big oak tree at the highest point of the village.

The image that remained the most vivid in the villagers' minds was the movement of the German soldiers as they marched precisely, in two's and three's, through the village. It seemed as if they were in a military parade, demonstrating their mercilessness and loyal discipline by denying their hearts even a glance at the beautiful girls watching them pass by. Their military demeanor was indisputable. However, there were times they showed their human side, as when they allowed the children to scrape the bottoms of their big pots with bare hands for a taste of the creamy chocolate residue.

During the two months of German occupation, time seemed suspended, for the bell-tower clock had stopped, hit by the first shot fired by a German soldier who wanted to make sure that he and his comrades had everyone's attention. Since then the hands of the clock had been frozen at 7:30 P.M., the moment when the Germans entered Toro. From that time on, the children played in the streets reluctantly.

Now people were counting the minutes until the arrival of the Allies. A day passed by, then two. Tired of waiting, the villagers began returning home, even though from time to time they heard shells exploding. At one point, a group of elderly people with a white flag started to move in the direction of the Allies. In this group was Nicola Ciaccia, who had been in the United States and knew some English. It was he who communicated to the Canadians to stop the hostilities because there were no Germans left in the village.

37 The VIII Army was composed of English, Indian, Moroccan, New Zealander, South African, Polish, and Canadian troops. The feeling of being liberated encouraged the villagers to come out into the streets, where they danced, sang, and embraced one another as if they had won the war. Soldiers threw chocolates and cigarettes from a jeep, while a huge black soldier escorted four women down the street, two under his right arm and two under his left. Children went after the soldiers for chocolate and other candies like mosquitoes mad for food. Some days later the Canadians liberated Campobasso.

On that occasion Marilena met a Canadian soldier named John, who would become the food supplier for the Albano family over the next few months. Hunger had become the true torment of the people, because the daily ration was a mere fifty grams of bread.

There was no electricity and no running water. This was

indeed the epoch of the survival of the fittest. To provide the barest essentials for daily living, people had to resort to all kinds of devious methods: black marketeering, prostitution, stealing. People were forced to sell everything they owned, from clothes to jewels. Without any scruple, Iuccio, like many others, turned to contraband for the survival of his family.

Widespread witch-hunting drove many of the fascists to hide in the hills or to relocate to places with the new communist ideology. But retaliation for his leadership role in the Party no longer worried Iuccio. It had been some time since he practiced his fascist views, that is to say, he refrained from the time the circumstances of war seemed unfavorable. He no longer participated in the assemblies and thus became subject to constant fascist vigilance. But the focus on him became less intensified following his child's misfortune in the farm machine accident, and then his mother's death.

However, the crowd, in exasperation, did attack some women who had collaborated with the Germans. They shaved the women's heads to mark their infidelity, parading them through the streets, insulting them, spitting on their faces, and kicking them. The truth was that some of them had been forced by their husbands into prostitution in order to feed their children.

Over time, certain events alerted the people to the cruel side of liberation. Unlike the German soldiers, some of the Allied soldiers, especially the Canadians and the Moroccans, were undisciplined; they seemed to have carte blanche to violate women. As a result of these rapes, children were born throughout Italy who possessed unusual physical characteristics, such as a strongly olive complexion, curly hair, or particularly fleshy lips. The liberation arrived at great cost. It seemed impossible to go to Heaven without going through the Hell of shame and dishonor first.

Iuccio felt betrayed by destiny for the second time, because his family had been divided again. He and Italo were liberated by the Allies while Benjamin was still under the German rule. Bad news continued to arrive, like the bad weather that year. Not even St. Peter's dome was spared, for it was struck by an incendiary bomb despite Rome's having been declared an "open city," meaning off limits. Rumors persisted that a German soldier in Rome, precisely at St. John's Square, had captured a whole company of disbanded Italian soldiers.

Iuccio remembered, after returning from Spain, the agony suffered by his children, who had asked him: "When will Mother come back?" Now his sense of guilt was destroying his mind. Once a romantic protagonist of the fascist revolution, he began to have constant remorse.

38

Iuccio had never had any reason to mistrust Angela, because she had devoted her body and soul to the whole family. But Ersilia Albano's frequent reminder of "away from the eyes, away from the heart" had created some doubts during the forced separation of the two spouses.

Contrary to Iuccio's doubts, Angela was in the land of the free. Despite the continuous compliments from the men in the war factory where she worked, she always managed to stand tall even though she did not have Penelope's skills in rejecting their demands.

She would then remember Iuccio's words on their wedding day: "I will protect you. I will take care of you. We will live together every minute of our lives. I will always love you and you will never suffer from loneliness." Angela remembered also the evenings when she and Iuccio would look at the stars together from their balcony, and she would point at one as theirs to gaze upon. When she looked at the star from America, she seemed to hear the sonorous melody of the crickets in the silence of the night and the barking of some dogs echoing from the neighboring farms.

Now those memories had haunted her. Although she prayed constantly that her family be spared, her conscience did bother her. She worried that her work in America might be contributing, even in the most remote way, to the endangerment of her family. Still, her service was necessary for her country; and even if she wanted to quit her position, somebody else would have taken her place.

She participated in everything that concerned the war, even lotteries initiated by fellow countrymen, to send foodstuff called "gift packages" to Italy, to be distributed among the most needy families. During Lent she would fast once a week and send her savings to the poor.

39 The noise of airplanes coming from Foggia toward Isernia, Venafro, and then Cassino was like a full river after a big storm. It would intensify little by little, filling the whole sky, deafening those people who were watching the show from below. As the war moved little by little toward Cassino, the Allies anticipated an easy undertaking.

One day Italo was having a good time watching the stream of vehicles of the VIII Army as it passed directly under his balcony en route to Cassino. After counting one hundred trucks, he became tired and switched to counting tanks, which fascinated him. Again he counted up to one hundred. Then bored, he began to greet the soldiers who saluted him from their turrets. He was also enjoying looking at the hundreds of airplanes, but was unable to count them.

Then Italo decided to visit the Canadian soldiers who were camped near a farm about three hundred meters on the other side of the road. He had often visited the soldiers because among them was John, whom Marilena had met and liked. On this particular day, as Italo was crossing the road, he lost a shoe. While he was retrieving it, a jeep driven by a Polish soldier hit him. John was among those who went to help. The driver put Italo on his jeep and transported him to the nearby Allied hospital, where he received immediate attention. After some minutes he regained his senses. The medics put twenty stitches in his scalp and the soldiers took him back home. Iuccio was advised to observe his son twenty-four hours a day because of the probability that Italo had suffered a concussion.

Several Canadian soldiers went often to see Italo, perhaps out of sympathy for his misfortune or his disfigured hand, perhaps for other reasons. They brought him many groceries, enough for the whole Albano family. Then, because they thought he was so cute, they had a uniform made for him, just like theirs, adopting him as their "mascot."

40 The famous monastery of Monte Cassino became an impregnable Teutonic Polyphemus, a one-eyed giant that mowed down Allied soldiers as farmers would harvest wheat. There were not enough Allied guns and airplanes to subdue its few German defenders. What worsened the situation was the inveterately bad weather. Mother Nature had formed a second enemy front against the Allies. It rained day after day, night after night, without abating. Then the temperature became polar, and it snowed continuously. The extreme cold was evidenced in the cracked hands of the poor soldiers, who, despite their Herculean efforts, saw only small successes while conquering thirty meters of bloody land and losing hundreds of lives in the effort.

The Germans were so well nested on that almost impervious mountain that the Allies took the only option remaining to them, to make the highest sacrifice—their lives. It was one of the bloodiest battles of that world conflict. In the past, earthquakes had almost destroyed Montecassino, leaving ruins in the mud. But this time among the rubble, semi-buried in the mud, there were now villagers: children, women and old men who had taken refuge in the old monastery. How cruel the law of this conflict seemed, that whoever killed first had the right to continue to breathe.

41

Iuccio had spent almost two years in anguish. Many things had happened since the last time he saw Benjamin. All the efforts to discover his whereabouts were in vain. Finally, unexpectedly, after so much agony, he and Italo saw Benjamin standing with a suitcase in front of the Albanos' house. Benjamin looked like a dusty white ghost, having lost a lot of weight. Iuccio embraced his son and the suitcase as if they were one, and with Italo they became entwined and immovable like a statue. Finally they looked at each other. Happiness and grief blended into unintelligible brutal cries. Italo had no chance to speak because of his father's nonstop questioning about his son's circumstances. The only word that came out of Benjamin was "prisoner."

When they arrived home, Mrs. Albano prepared a magnificent supper. Each took his place at the table at once; but in Francesco's place there was now John, Marilena's Canadian fiancé. In Benjamin's mind, John resembled his tall blond German oppressors; in reality, he was the complete opposite. The supper that they were about to eat was the consequence of his generosity. It was a beautiful party, a wonderful night, and Benjamin said nothing about his dislike for John. He would talk only about his work in the concentration camp, which consisted of cleaning and cutting potatoes.

42

One day in the village of Toro, after the hostilities had ended, Francesco received a totally unexpected package from his father. In it he found a beautiful gold Bulova watch, six cartons of Chesterfields, shoes, and a suit, the first gifts he had ever received in his life. He wasted no time in selling three of the cartons of cigarettes at the black-market price. With the profits he asked two childhood friends, Attilio and Tonio, to join him in experiencing the nightlife of a big spender by going to one of Campobasso's famous cabarets. They sat at a table where they were served like true gentlemen, smoking the prestigious American cigarettes from which came a seductive aroma.

For Francesco, however, this new life after war was not satisfying. Because there was a good chance that Italy would end up under the Soviet hegemony, he thought every day about America, where he felt that his real future was.

43 It was March 19, 1946. Iuccio, Benjamin, and Italo arrived at Francesco's house by carriage from Campobasso where they were guests at what was called "Saint Joseph's Poor Man's Dinner." This is a day dedicated to feeding the poor. Many families had to feed at least three people of the community: a man, a woman and a child, representing Joseph, Mary and Jesus. Immediately Iuccio complimented Aunt Maria, exclaiming, "Ah, I smell the aroma of beans of the past!"

Attilio, Francesco's friend, was also a guest at this traditional religious dinner. Knowing that Iuccio liked politics, he asked him about what was being said in Campobasso concerning the imminent referendum. Was Italy going to be a monarchy or a republic?

Iuccio, who had lived on politics in the past, immediately declared that he was no longer interested in the art of politics. "From now on I am interested only in getting the authorization from the American government for my children and me and Francesco, hoping that the four of us will be able to depart together."

To that, Attilio proposed a toast for great success in the immediate future and added, "With all my heart I wish all of you well, and I also wish that when you arrive in that blessed land, you will do me the favor of sending me a one-way ticket." All lifted their glasses in agreement. Francesco raised his glass too, but it was obvious that something was bothering him.

Francesco had received a letter from his father, who was discouraging him from aspiring to the land of opportunity. Joseph, his father, had written, among other things, "America is a harsh land, not suitable for everyone, especially for students. This is still a pretty wild environment, more so than Siberia or the Argentinean Pampas, that devours whoever enters, and it is impossible to master this bastard language."

In that letter his father continued to justify his logic, describing the tragic fate of some Italian emigrants of his time. He spoke about a young Abruzzese, Pasquale d'Angelo, who was known as "the poet of the pick and shovel." He had come to America at the age of sixteen and died young from starvation. During the icy days of winter, the young poet could stay warm only by remaining in bed, without a piece of bread.

Then Joseph, Francesco's father, had mentioned a certain Arturo Giovannitti, a fellow townsman from Campobasso, who, despite being one of the greatest writers of the century, faced the possibility of the electric chair, having been accused of anarchism and saved only by his eloquent self-defense and a poem called "The Walker." On January 12, 1912, he had headed the famous labor strike in Lawrence, Massachusetts, an important manufacturing city. He and Charles Tresca, another labor leader born in Abruzzo, had walked the streets with thousands of men and women carrying posters with messages like "Bread and Roses," meaning that they wanted jobs, but with dignity.

In defending himself in that Salem court Giovannitti had said, "I learned at my mother's knee to revere the name of the republic.... I ask the district attorney, who speaks about the 'New England tradition', what he means by that—if he means the New England tradition of this same town where they once burned witches at the stake, or does he mean the New England tradition of those men who dumped the tea in Boston Harbor and refused to continue under the iron heel of the British authority.... And if it be that these hearts of ours must be stilled on the same death chair, and by the same current of fire that has destroyed the life of the wife murderer and the patricide and parricide, then I say that tomorrow we shall pass into greater judgment, that tomorrow we shall go from your presence into a Presence where history shall give its last word to us."

His father's letter continued negatively, also mentioning the infamous case of Sacco and Vanzetti, who were executed in the electric chair and later recognized as innocent of their alleged crime. He ended the letter with these words: "Dear Son, Discrimination and racism are felt in the poisoned air against us Italians. If you come, this will be your *Via Dolorosa* (Way to your Cross)."

Francesco was not interested in all these stories, true or false. He was certain of one thing only: it was obvious that his father did not know him. His father did not know that his son, from the time he was a child, had assumed his father's role, reaping wheat at harvesting time, harvesting grapes in October, and gathering olives in November.

After supper, Francesco gave the letter to Iuccio, who read it quickly and then reassured Francesco that the three of them would not depart without him. Moreover, Iuccio went to Rome several times to see a childhood friend, Angelo Pifalo, soliciting his help with their applications to America.

As hoped, within one year, all four obtained their visas and passports and set the date for their departure.

On the next Election Day, the people rejected the monarchy in favor of a democratic republic. Now Francesco felt only a benign, sweet breeze blowing toward the West.

44 The evening before their departure, Francesco went throughout the village to get one last look at everything that was familiar to him. It had rained a little, and in the dark of the night, the stones shone as

if to facilitate his walk, to show him the way through the unlighted streets.

First he visited the small church of Saint Rocco, the mecca for many pilgrims in ancient times before it was part of the village. Then he visited the main church, a place of thousands of childhood memories, where on a holiday he would go to ring the melodious bells. Finally, he arrived at the monastery, the source of many beautiful cultural experiences, of recitals and plays. Leaving that dear world was painful, but not cause for regret.

Very early in the morning of May 18, 1947, before dawn, the sky was so clear that one could see many places from the balcony. Relatives began to come first, silently, as if they were going to a funeral. Then his friends came, speaking in low voices. Lastly came the whole neighborhood, a bit more spirited. In that early morning the faces around Francesco were pale from the excitement of the departure. Francesco himself was overcome by emotion.

The time to say goodbye to dear ones had arrived. He had to face the trauma of separation now. Aunt Maria, as they called Francesco's mother, gave out anguished cries, accompanied by invocations to God of "poor child of mine, protect him." He embraced his sisters and then his mother. It seemed that the end of a drama was being played. Neither he nor they could detach from each other until the faithful friends, Attilio and Tonio, a bit boisterous, intervened and accompanied him to the square, where his brother-in-law Saverio was waiting with a two-wheeled cart, on which they had already put his suitcase.

Francesco, still mute from the evening before, turned around for one last affectionate look at everybody in that square where he had played so many games. Saverio lashed the horse once, and slowly they left that ancient world.

Waiting for him at the train station were Iuccio, Benjamin and Italo, all with big smiles and without any sign of tears. Even Marilena arrived with all her family. Seeing Francesco so distressed, she approached and comforted him affectionately, embracing him with a prolonged kiss bathed by tears that slowly slipped to their moistened lips. Then whispering in his ear quietly, she said, "Write to me." Francesco nodded, still unable to speak. As the train departed, the four travelers gave one last look at Monforte Castle, soaked by the first dazzling rays of the sun. Below, the city, shaded by dawn, was still resting.

When they arrived at the port of Naples, the ship welcomed them with a fanfare that added to the shouts and the cries before the *Saturnia* departed. Francesco stood looking toward the east, while Iuccio, Benjamin and Italo looked toward the west.

45 For the four of them the Atlantic Ocean seemed vast, until now existing only as the one in Pinocchio's fable in which the enormous shark swallowed Geppetto. Now it was real; the sea was so immense that it seemed endless, and it showed its cruel side. On a dark, cloudy, very windy morning, while they were out on deck looking at the waves as big as mountains beating against the ship, a powerful wave suddenly swallowed Francesco, Benjamin and Italo, who landed on their backs, wet and terrorized.

For almost the whole journey, however, the sweet and clear spring sky was broken only by a few clouds. Seductive songs such as "Brazil" made everyone easily forget any apprehensions they had concerning their long oceanic crossing. The ship offered a variety of diversions: a big dining room that became a ballroom in the evening, a theater, a tobacco shop, a small library, billiards, and other attractions. It was a gentleman's life, free as a bird, without a worry, enjoying the weather, the food, the music and the theater at night.

After a couple of days, Francesco had overcome the painful feelings of separation from his family and for the first time was having a good time, a true vacation. Benjamin had lost control of himself and was enjoying life as if it were the last day on earth. Every night he danced, at times the jitterbug, at others the boogie-woogie. He was surrounded by beautiful girls, who were attracted to him. Nobody knew where he had learned to dance so well as to be able to send all those girls into some kind of frenzy. He danced with them continuously, moving them around as if they were dolls. Maybe he had seen a film of the great Fred Astaire. One thing was certain: he didn't learn that in school or as a prisoner of war.

Throughout the journey, the boys were free to come and go as they pleased. The last evening on the ship, Iuccio met Francesco before supper as he had always done on this trip. He could not hide his apprehension anymore and confessed his concerns. "I have to admit that I am very worried about Benjamin. Have you noticed his strange behavior? He has been disappearing from morning until evening, and I see him drinking too much beer!"

"What do you expect?" Francesco answered. "We are young and free for the first time, and we feel like wild horses in an open field. You frightened me. I thought that you were having some serious problems."

When Benjamin and Italo arrived, they all took a seat at their table for their last dinner on board.

About 4:00 in the afternoon of May 25, after seven days, one could see land far away with buildings sprouting like so many stalks of asparagus. The ship, with its siren, started to announce its arrival at the city that later would be known as the "Big Apple." Soon they saw the Statue of Liberty, and passengers waved their white handkerchiefs as if the sorceress Circe had seduced them. Was this only a marvelous dream or was it true?

The *Saturnia* slowly approached the pier, where a large crowd was waiting, among them Angela, accompanied by her father-in-law. There was much joy. Passengers tried to recognize dear ones, who were waiting anxiously, often applauding or making signs with their hands to attract their attention.

The disembarking began, one by one, under the magical Empire State Building. First-class passengers went first—

women, children and men. In that same order followed those of second and third class. The inseparable four were almost the last ones to touch ground.

Benjamin and Italo ran to their mother, while Iuccio went toward his father. They remained embraced for some time with much sobbing and many tears. Then it was Francesco's turn to greet his cousin and Grandfather Totti.

They went to a beautiful restaurant where they could talk and update one another on so many things. Angela was flanked by her two angels on one side of the table, while Iuccio, Grandfather Totti, and Francesco sat on the opposite side. The new arrivals had never seen so much food, but the worry and the strong desire for food now belonged to the past.

At dusk, the neon lights became a spectacular show, lighting the great, tall buildings, offering advertising for Coca-Cola and other products. It all seemed an optical illusion. Francesco then thought about the single light in the kitchen of his house, pale as death itself, barely illuminating the entrances to the other rooms, one in which slept his mother and sisters, and the other that he shared with his grandfather. This was his old world, the source of a thousand childhood memories, the hearth where, during the winter months, he would hear stories of Greeks and Romans, Saracens and Normans, but also of witches and goblins.

46 That first evening in America, the four were guests of Dr. Alfredo Santillo, Iuccio's childhood friend, who had left for America as an expatriate in 1935, as did his exiled twin brother who had gone to Spain for the same anti-fascist ideals.

Dr. Santillo's house was large, with a green garden dotted by many fountains and statues, and a swimming pool nearby. Near the patio stood a pergola under which was prepared a long table full of cheeses, ham, bread, and many bottles of regular and sparkling wine.

"Welcome, welcome," the good physician said, embracing first his old friend Iuccio and then all the others. When he introduced his mother, Donna Rosina, she went to meet Grandfather Totti, speaking to him in the dialect of their mother tongue. They had gone to elementary school together in their village half a century ago. At the sound of Donna Rosina's voice, Francesco had the sensation of hearing his own mother speaking. For a moment his imagination took him back to Italy, making him forget that he was just a few footsteps away from skyscrapers. On this serene night in May, one could clearly see on the water the upside-down reflection of these tall buildings. It was as if they wanted to reach the depths of the sea as well as the distant sky.

Donna Rosina liked Francesco immediately, because he seemed to be unpretentious. The dog was barking in a festive mood, and after a few minutes he was walking freely among the guests, as if he, too, had known them for some time.

As soon as they sat down at the table, Iuccio began dominating the conversation. He spoke about Spain, where, under strange circumstances, he had seen the doctor's twin brother, the pharmacist, who had opened Iuccio's eyes to his blindly embraced fascist ideology.

Alfredo had much respect for his old friend, but he had to interrupt him. "Dear Compare Iuccio, you have gone through hell in your recent past. You had such a tempestuous past and you deserve a happy future. This is a generous land, where one can pretty much control his destiny, with a system that works rather well, especially for the weak and the defenseless, as most immigrants are. There are many opportunities for everybody, even if one must begin from zero, as all of us had to do. I like this system a lot because there is no limit to one's progress. This is a land of self-determination."

Francesco, the oldest of the three youths, was curious, and wanted the good doctor to say more. Pretending not to understand, he asked, "Excuse me, Doctor, what does that long word mean—self-determination?"

The doctor was happy to elaborate. "This is a country

born by itself, without the help of a midwife, where self-reliance is a way of life. It was conceived in the form of many free states, each different from the other, where the individual can operate freely while aiming to reach the top of the ladder."

Francesco, spellbound, had an insatiable thirst for information, and encouraged Dr. Santillo to continue.

"Well, let me explain it to you. America is like a pyramid, at the base of which is the largest mass of people. These poor, hungry, hard-working laborers are its true wealth. Their freedom to operate gives them hope to reach the top of the pyramid." The doctor then took a dollar out of his pocket and showed Francesco the pyramid pictured on the reverse side of the bill. "In short, this base is where the action is, where the transactions are concluded, where the citizens, not the powers above as in other nations, resolve their own problems. This is a populist country, where justice is administered by the people, because the greatest number of the magistrates are elected by the people. And the laws are equal for everybody, including the president himself. In other words, problems are solved at local levels and not in Washington, except in the case of war when everything is decided from high above. The system protects the weak and the oppressed against the strong and despotic."

The conversation was exciting, but they all felt tired, beginning to yawn like fish out of water gasping for air. Mrs. Santillo, the doctor's wife, interrupted. "Young people are not interested in long speeches; rather, let us talk about tomorrow's plans."

"Tomorrow, early in the morning we will take the train to continue our journey," Iuccio responded.

"No, no," interrupted the doctor. "I have canceled all my appointments so that I can be at your complete disposal. I would not like you to miss this opportunity to see our city. We will go by car on a beautiful sight-seeing trip." Considering the subject closed, he handed Angela the telephone, suggesting she tell her mother that they were postponing their departure for one day.

But before the guests retired, the good doctor wanted to

show them his Fido's intelligence. "Say good night in Italian to our guests!"

"Bawa, bawa."

"Fold your paws!" The dog lay down, putting one leg over the other. And so with laughter they all went to their rooms.

The next day, after an abundant breakfast, they went downtown. It seemed as if they had arrived in a wonderland. Big green parks had merry-go-rounds and many trees flanked by benches where some people read and rested. Others hurried to catch underground trains, almost in a fury as if they were in a labyrinth. The streets had four-lane highways. There were theaters, cinemas, high-fashion shops, and supermarkets. Some store windows displayed electric razors and battery-run radios.

In this complex scene, among thousands of busy people rushing among all the buildings, one could easily lose his identity. Francesco was experiencing this phenomenon of feeling lonely among so many people. It was a uniquely strange sensation for him. Yet the immense space also gave him a feeling of boundless freedom. It did not seem likely that from such humble origins the four could suddenly have found a way to reach the stars. Perhaps it was only a city, but it was one where the impossible became possible.

The doctor tried to explain to them that there was a big Italian imprint left in the heart of many American cities. "It is a long story," he began. "Many of these buildings and even the underground, metropolitan transportation system were constructed by immigrants, mostly Italians. In fact, in 1890, ninety percent of the public jobs in this city were held by Italians. A city official once said, 'We cannot get along without the Italians.' The official added, 'We want them to do the dirty jobs that the Irishmen do not want to do anymore.' An American historian cared to say that the greatest metropolis in the world rose from the sweat and misery of Italian labor."

Their friend also pointed out that technology did not always succeed in dominating nature. "In fact, on March 12, 1888, New York City was paralyzed by a heavy snowfall, saved only by the shovels put in motion by the muscles of Italians. People were waiting for spring, when suddenly a storm buried the city under three feet of snow, leaving thousands of people stranded and animals abandoned on the roads. With strong incentives the government was able to gather thousands of Italian immigrants who, while shoveling the snow, discovered some four hundred frozen bodies. This violent act of nature forced politicians to build tunnels through the city for the future trains and subways so that the city would not be prey to nature again."

When they had completed their tour of the downtown area, it was almost noon, and they hurried back home, where Isabella had prepared a sumptuous lunch. While they were eating, the telephone rang. It was Angela's mother, Assunta, begging them to come as soon as possible because there were many people waiting for them.

About 3:00 in the afternoon, they all took the train to Ohio. Despite the many distractions and amazing sights during the trip, Benjamin and Italo did not leave their mother for one minute, but kissed her and caressed her repeatedly.

They crossed the state of Pennsylvania and marveled at the mountains, woods, animals, and vast expanses of wheat and corn. The surrounding hills were dotted by many small farms where cows and sheep grazed. Francesco had some idea of this land, but not one that promised to be a new Eden. These images did not correspond to those preconceived in Italy, where he had known only one American family, Giovanni the baker, his wife and his two children, Pezzi and Maichi, with the latter spending much of his time playing his violin. Everyone in Giovanni's family was in good health, and none of them thought of working in the fields. Francesco therefore had the impression that all Americans were rich, but not interested in farming.

He had known a number of American soldiers at the end of the war, all tall and generous to children with their chocolates and to adults with their cigarettes. He had also seen some violent, but fascinating films of the American Far West, featuring Indians, and cowboys or desperados hoping to become rich looking for gold. But he had never imagined that America was the heaven on earth that they were now observing from the train. Everything still seemed a magical dream.

Finally, around eleven o'clock in the evening, the persistent train whistles announced the arrival at the final stop, Youngstown station, where Mr. Ceppone, his wife Assunta, and her brother Joseph, Francesco's father, were waiting for them. Among the crowd one could hear the grandparents' joyous cries and sobbing while Joseph called to his son, whom he had not seen in fourteen years. They all took turns to embrace and kiss, happy to be reunited at last.

47 During the first weeks, Francesco became acquainted with his new surroundings. The America that he observed did not seem at all the environment described by his father in that scary letter a year ago. What he saw gave him a true sense of peace and tranquillity. The door of every house was always open, and in the morning the newspapers were on the lawns. On the porches one could see bottles of milk, just delivered by the milkman. The feeling of being in a safe place was a reality, without the vicious fascist control using threats and oppression. His father's pessimism, which had described violence, recrimination, hatred and abuses by some Americans, belonged to the past. Life now seemed simple, easy to face.

Like magic, the houses had running water, hot and cold; no one had to get it from the wells as they did in his village. Every ten minutes buses departed from a nearby station. There were parks where children played, several sports fields, and efficient offices where one never had to wait in line for bureaucratic reasons. It was astounding to see the banks executing transactions in the blink of an eye. Theaters and museums were always crowded, and every city had a symphony orchestra.

Everything was efficient and carried out with a correctness designed to convince the most lawless person to change his ways and pursue the right path. Traffic was orderly, with rarely a horn sounding off, even without the supervision of a police officer. Likewise, the vast cemeteries were orderly, green and well kept, bringing dignity to death in an eternal resting garden. The system mirrored the simplicity of a varied but united people. Birth ranks did not exist as in the old European society, to affirm the purity or the impurity of one's blood. The code of inequality did not seem to exist as it had in the Old World, especially in the fascist hierarchical cobweb.

Only a two-party political system existed, with two distinct philosophies that complemented each other, each party looking over the other's shoulders. This bipartisan system could be explained in simple terms: the Democratic Party tended to protect the common man; the more conservative Republicans tended to curb public expenses. Yet, there were no assemblies or political demonstrations in the squares.

Francesco saw the Old World as complicated, tired of living, almost dying. Nothing worked. The New World was full of energy and sure of itself and of its future. Indeed it was a land of hope.

The general sense of security was based on the idea that respect for the individual, for the man next door, is of utmost importance. That sense of harmony perhaps evolved from the fusion of many cultures. In appearance, Americans seemed about the same, but in actuality one knew that they came from many different lands. In Francesco's neighborhood one could hear many languages—Greek, Polish, Italian, Russian, Slovak, and Spanish, for example—and all lived in perfect harmony, a microcosm of the whole world. *E Pluribus Unum.*

Francesco saw an orderly, pleasant land, offering him a future to inspire hope in the American Dream. He did not lack ambition; therefore, the desire to master the language became his top priority.

48

As a fascist fanatic, Iuccio had often contributed to spreading the wrong image about America. Now, Iuccio also felt overpowered by the beauties of this new world. He admired its practicality, a true American virtue, but especially the modesty of its citizens, who seemed to live their lives in complete accordance with the Gospel, "Whoever exalts himself will be humbled, and whoever humbles himself will be exalted."

There were no castles or big villas inhabited by princes, barons, counts, or anyone with such noble titles. The churches, built like wooden barracks, especially in Italian neighborhoods, lacked the magnificence of the sumptuous edifices in Italy. The simplicity of the people who attended these plain churches could be mistaken for crudeness by those who did not look beyond the surface. There were few religious holidays and Mass was never solemn. There were no bands to parade the saint throughout the city, no fireworks to accompany it. The priests and all the prelates seemed to be common men. Some churches, not being Catholic, even had married priests, mirroring the diversity of religious groups.

Iuccio revealed to Francesco that he was happy about the decision that he had made. Above all he was happy for his children, who seemed to feel that they were in Heaven, always near their mother, never tiring of her affection. When he thought about the past, all those years of late-night living, escapades and intense passion, when he kept on living with a sense of *mea culpa* for his betrayal of his innocent and naive wife, he would actually shiver at these thoughts and feel guilty all over again.

He feared not finding a job, perhaps because of his lack of manual skills. He was also afraid of the ghosts of his past, especially those fascist ones. Looking for a job seemed almost illegal for him; he was afraid that they'd find out about his past. What he did not know was that his papers were in order, and that the Constitution protected him from the fascist past, as he was now a legal immigrant.

On more than one occasion, Iuccio observed that all his fellow townsmen, with minimal education and no political ideology, had reached an enviable economic position, breaking the cycle of poverty that had forced them to live as slaves in Italy. He saw clearly that almost all Italians in America acted like industrious ants during the summer and not like lazy cicadas; they had learned to work a lot and talk a little.

Iuccio decided to apply at several consulates—Detroit, Cleveland, Philadelphia, and New Orleans—for a clerk position, the only work for which he felt qualified. But he knew that finding a job wouldn't be easy. Angela, however, continued to encourage him, telling him not to worry. Keeping the whole family together was the important thing for her. That would assure her true happiness, and her job would take care of the rest. Iuccio, on the other hand, thought that the real passport to a dignified life would be a job. Giovanni Mazzarino, a friend of the Ceppones, told him once, "Dear friend, in America one cannot continue to dream by sprinkling hopes with water. What empowers you here are your muscles, that is to say, 'Take any job as long as you work.'"

Angela had never been a protester, but she reacted immediately in her husband's defense. "My husband has never worked with his hands, and he certainly will not have any need to do so as long as I am alive. The place for him is in an office."

Mr. Mazzarino made a sign with his hands as if to apologize and left them. As soon as he arrived home, he vented his feelings with his wife. "The fascists, the new arrivals, want to boss people even in America, but they will not do it here. I have told them that only sweating with your hands will let you earn a living in this country."

"What do you care if the fascists work with their hands, their feet, or their heads?" answered his disgusted wife, letting him know that she was interested only in what was going on in her own house.

But her husband persisted. "This is important to me,

because, here, we—the common people, the peasants, as they call us—have the power."

Iuccio's doubts about finding employment grew day by day. Was Mr. Mazzarino right? Iuccio realized that intellectual ability counted a lot, but one had to know the language, which had been his most effective tool in the past, the essence of his identity. However, he had always been completely opposed to learning English, having hated it for most of his life.

Fortunately Iuccio was no longer the man he had once been. The change in him was like night and day. He clearly understood that the way he had lived in Italy was of little use in America. In Italy he had lived a hedonist's life of politics, power, and passion for pretty women. Now his only passion was for his family. He never missed Mass with his family, and he wanted to make a future for himself with deeds, not just words. He was determined to learn a trade and leave behind the old habits and, above all, the old ambitions.

49 Immigrants' children, especially those of the first generation of large families, had a rather myopic vision of the future, often leaving school to find jobs to help at home. The Italians who arrived in later years were different, perhaps more aggressive and better educated. Francesco, Benjamin, and Italo were more ambitious than their predecessors, attending summer school to learn English so that they could enroll in school in the fall.

On the first of July, the teacher informed the class, which was made up entirely of immigrants, that schools would be closed for two days to celebrate the important historical event that had taken place on July 4, 1776, in Philadelphia. He encouraged them to participate in the ceremonies and parades for the occasion, which celebrated the proclaiming of the Declaration of Independence for the American colonies. "Here, patriotic holidays are celebrated more than religious ones because this is a land of few saints," explained the teacher.

There was no doubt about American patriotism on this holiday. The lawns of every house were decorated with the Stars and Stripes. Several bands played John Philip Sousa's songs. At the head of the parade on the main road were two men with fifes and a boy with drums, playing music of the era, representing the Spirit of 1776, when a few revolutionaries, with little knowledge of the martial arts of the time, challenged the inherited power of the stronger British army, their oppressors.

The trio of musicians, dressed in eighteenth-century uniforms, was followed by majorettes, made up of public- and private-school girls. The parade continued with antique cars, tanks, firemen with their latest equipment, and veterans representing the Army, Navy, Air Force, and Marines. Then there were dignitaries and politicians, representing different ideologies.

For Francesco this parade was the confirmation of his observations of a people who believe in a constitution that guarantees rights to everybody. Iuccio's response, on the other hand, was marred by the unhappiness of his personal situation. After his first positive reactions, he began to see America as a monster, a Minotaur that hid violence, racism, and cynicism behind an egalitarian façade. When he voiced this opinion, he often provoked scorn and anger within his family and opposition from whoever listened to him.

The day after this patriotic celebration, the teacher was eager to know whether the future citizens had any questions about the weekend festivities. A student let the teacher know that she had not seen Indians or blacks in the parade. "Weren't they also free to participate?"

"Certainly," the teacher answered. "From the very beginning, when the War of Independence started, even though the blacks were then slaves, they have played an important role in our history. As a matter of fact, of the two hundred thousand soldiers who participated in that war, five thousand were black."

He continued, "The Revolution may actually have begun on March 5, 1770, when a slave by the name of Crispus Attucks, who earlier had escaped from his owner, was one of the first to die for the cause of independence. He was killed when some English soldiers, frightened by the crowds that were pelting them with snowballs, opened fire on the people. The farmers called that cowardly act the Boston Massacre. When on July 4 the Continental Congress approved the resolution that all men are created equal, all the blacks interpreted such a declaration as a manifesto of liberty for all the oppressed." However, slavery remained legal in America for many decades.

The class learned not just English that day, but some history as well.

50 That summer school operated until the first of August with positive results. But the first Monday of September, Labor Day, was a disappointment. This event struck them as strange, since most of the world celebrated it on the first of May. A few minutes after the parade started, gusts of wind, with hail and ice, forced everyone to take refuge in several stores and restaurants. An aged Italian, who was enjoying the ceremony next to Iuccio, told him that the unusual behavior of the squirrels, running here and there as if they had gone crazy and the birds, chirping more than the usual, signaled a mini-hurricane.

According to tradition, the academic year for both private and public schools did not begin until after Labor Day. Both Benjamin and Italo were sent to a private high school in New Rochelle, New York, run by Salesian priests, while Francesco enrolled in a local public high school that was less severe, less regimented than the private ones, but equally interesting in many aspects.

The first week of school was intense for Francesco, who was submerged in a cascade of general rules. A school counselor, after a preliminary oral evaluation, had placed him, now nineteen years old, in the ninth grade.

Although everything was going well for Francesco, he still felt nostalgic for his homeland, for family, and for his many friends. Soon, however, he began to feel part of the system, which was practical and progressive. All the teachers, especially those who communicated in Italian with him, encouraged him. And recognizing how awkward he felt among his much younger classmates, they did their best to support him.

Dr. Parenti, the principal, assured Francesco that he would speak on his behalf to all the teachers who were trying to facilitate his study of English. He also promised to provide Francesco with an interpreter to minimize any misunderstanding in the future. All these courtesies and sensibilities on the part of the school staff indeed gave Francesco hope for a rosy future that some Americans called the American Dream.

One afternoon Francesco was summoned by Dr. Parenti, who wanted to introduce him to the interpreter he had promised. To his surprise, the interpreter was a girl of about seventeen years, the daughter of Italians who spoke a form of dialect. She was a refined and kind young lady of enormous modesty and self-control. Her name was Grace. The principal explained that if in the future there were difficulties during the day, his office would be at their disposal. Then he asked Grace to give the new arrival a tour of the school to acquaint him with the grounds.

The two left the main entrance where the administrative offices were. Grace began explaining in an Italian dialect that classes for seniors were held on the first floor and those for sophomores and juniors were on the second and third floors. Then she showed him the theater, the auditorium, and the library, which held thousands of books. There were many small classrooms with seats for no more than thirty students, and on every teacher's desk there were family photos. Finally, there was a large cafeteria for students and teachers. They then went out to see the rest of the campus, where the young guide showed him tennis courts and fields for football and soccer. Nearby was also a covered swimming pool and a *palestra* for basketball.

All of this amazed Francesco, who recalled how

miserable his former world was, how poor the small schoolyard where with friends he had improvised soccer games. There were no libraries, no cafeterias, no central heat, not even drinking water fountains with overcrowded classrooms.

At the end he asked her if he could accompany her home, which was about a kilometer from the school. She accepted very willingly but asked him to hurry the pace in order to arrive home on time, before nightfall. On the way, they could hear the choir of the crickets, suggesting a rural atmosphere that reminded him of his native land.

Suddenly, Grace asked him about the war, in a dialect that sounded like beautiful music to Francesco's ears. But the memories of guns and the terrible noise that they had made, the thunder made by falling buildings hit by heavy artillery, and the screams of wounded children were still very painful.

"You can't understand," answered her new Italian friend. Grace remained silent. Then, seeing the sadness visible on his face, she changed the subject. "I don't understand the word *lei*."

"Oh, it means 'you'," replied Francesco, obviously relieved to be discussing something else.

"Then what is the difference between *lei*, *tu*, and *voi*?" she pursued.

"Well, the meaning is the same, and while *tu* is used with people you know very well, *lei* is used to address people whom you do not know well. Use *voi* to be respectful."

"Oh," Grace said, "I have studied French. Perhaps the idea is the same—*tu* and *voi* are like the French *tu* and *vous*."

"Exactly," he responded.

"*Alors, tutoyons-nous*," said she.

"I am happy that you studied French. But why not Italian?" asked Francesco.

"I am sorry. I would have liked to, but Italian is not in our curriculum," she responded.

"Why not?"

"Because it is not required."

The two walked along for a while in the semidarkness,

absorbed in their own thoughts. Then, breaking the silence, she said, "I have to tell you that you are very different from other young men that I know."

"In what sense am I different?"

"For one, your manner of speaking—always calm. Then you dress in a mature fashion with your white shirt and tie. As you probably noticed, only teachers dress like you. Your face is always shaved and your hair nicely combed. But what I admire most about you is your inquisitive spirit."

Francesco, a bit embarrassed, tried to thank her, but since the right words wouldn't come out, he became silent.

She took advantage of his pause to return to the subject of their earlier conversation and what seemed to be the closest thing to her heart. "Certainly I cannot understand the war as you lived it. Here we never had to worry about being attacked, being bombed, or being hungry. But there was a war here, too."

Francesco looked at her, puzzled. "I would really like to know how you spent that time, how you lived that period."

"Well," she began, "until now I have never found the courage to speak about it, but for some strange reason I don't feel embarrassed confiding in you. Ours was rather a psychological bombardment, but not from the enemy."

"I am sorry, but I don't follow you," he said.

"We are Americans, born in this country, which I love like my mother. My brother enlisted in the Marines, and he was sent to fight in the Pacific, where he saw many of his companions die. Our patriotism and loyalty to this land have been like those of other nationalities, if not better. Despite our great efforts and complete dedication and devotion to this land, we Italian-Americans have been humiliated and given little respect. We have been considered suspicious, insulted with gestures and intolerable discrimination, and derided as fascists and other offending and degrading words." Clearly excited, she paused to catch her breath before continuing.

"We were declared 'enemy aliens' by our government and the police. They imposed a curfew on us, and we could not travel farther than five miles. Even our radios were confiscated. This racist *modus operandi* gave some of us an inferiority complex."

By now he was very curious and encouraged her to go on.

"During that time, more than ten thousand Italians were forced to leave their homes and were confined in various camps like the one in Missoula, Montana—just as the Nazis did with the Jews. At the same time, our brothers, serving in the war, were dying with the Stars and Stripes on their uniforms. There were even some well-known personalities among the Italian victims, such as the father of Joe Di Maggio, the most famous baseball player in the country. The government confiscated his fishing boats and caused him a major crisis."

Francesco was seeing another face of America from a persuasive source, from the mouth of a very beautiful girl, and he felt struck by lightning. His puzzled look prompted her to continue. "Even Enzo Pinza, who sang in the famous Metropolitan Opera, was arrested and interned in a camp in New Jersey. During these terrible times thousands of Italians and Italian-Americans lost their jobs. Half a million Italian-Americans were forced to carry an ID card at all times. Then there were the terrible stories of ordinary people like Rosina Trova, who received the message from the Navy that her son had been killed at Pearl Harbor, while at the same time she received a letter classifying her as an enemy alien. As you can see, bigotry and civil paranoia made people suspicious of Italians."

They had arrived at her home. He thanked her for her company and asked her if they could meet again tomorrow at the same time.

Francesco spent the whole night thinking about that shameful page of American history. It had shattered the beautiful image that he had created in his mind about a country where justice, freedom, and perfection reigned. For the first time, Francesco felt something negative about America, and this new feeling bothered him.

While in school the next day, he did not even go to the

cafeteria for lunch, as he had always done before. Instead, he went to the library, hoping to find a friend he could confide in, but he knew one. So he decided to write to a friend in Italy. Although he fully intended to write about the doubts caused by Grace's comments about America, the letter turned out differently:

Dear Attilio,

I hope that you have received my letters in which I spoke to you about many things and the many provocative girls I have met. They wear short dresses and short shorts. What is more, they go arm in arm with boys and kiss in the open, without anyone being scandalized, with their hair extremely short as if to show their rebellion against traditions, et cetera.

Now I am anxious to give you the latest news. I have met a girl completely different from those already described. She is attractive, modest, elegant, refined, of a rare sweetness, perhaps sent to me by God himself. During that short time I spent with her, I have seen in her so many good qualities. I seem to be in complete harmony with her. One of her sentences in particular has impressed me the most. She and I were talking about the character of a person when she forcefully said: "To me, ethics are more important than aesthetics. The external impression left by people is not the kind and genuine one of the soul." Her internal characteristics seem to be complemented by her beautiful external ones. I have to go to my favorite history class at this time.

Regards to everybody,
Francesco

Grace's talk had made Francesco more cautious, as if his new experience had suddenly matured him, causing him to reevaluate his favorable first impressions of America. Later, and with some disappointment, he talked to friends about his thoughts. He also mentioned his feelings to Iuccio, who responded, "You have always called me a pessimist. Now you are hearing the same arguments from a more objective source. Finally you understand that you cannot trust these wild people who are not yet completely civilized."

51

Despite feelings of uncertainty, Francesco was enjoying life. He had been able to rise to the challenges at school with Grace's diligent help. More than ever, he wanted to succeed.

Mr. Conti, his history teacher, clearly understood his pupil's fascination with American history and seized every opportunity to tell him about the architects of the country's social hierarchy, that historical pyramid about which Dr. Santillo had first spoken. "Those whom we call the Founding Fathers—Washington, Adams, Madison, and Jefferson, and others like Franklin, who 'stole lightning from the skies and the scepter from the tyrants,' as a French epigrammatist once said—were all worried about the abuse of power. They believed that absolute power corrupts absolutely, denying people a prosperous life. You see," explained Mr. Conti, "your liberty has its roots in these wise men who tried to protect the future generations. When people are abused by a politician, it means that they allowed him."

These words resonated in the mind of Francesco, who recalled Mussolini asking, "How is it possible, in a nation of servants, not to become its master?"

After school the following day, Francesco and Grace met as planned in front of the principal's office. It was she who greeted him first. "Hello, how did it go today?"

"*Meglio del primo giorno.*"

"No, no, no. Answer me in English."

"Better than the first day."

"Good, very good," she said. But their conversation in English ended there. His vocabulary was still too limited to continue the dialogue.

"Can we go to the cafeteria to drink a Coke?" he asked, resorting to Italian.

"Certainly. I am just as thirsty as you."

While they sipped their drinks, she told him that her parents knew about their arrangement and were eager to meet him.

"I, too, would like to meet them when it is convenient for you. If you want, I could accompany you home today."

She thought for a few seconds. "Wait for me here. I want to tell my friends that I am not going back with them as usual."

While Francesco was waiting, a black student started speaking to him. But Francesco was not listening, because he was busy staring at the young man's astonishingly white teeth. When Grace came back, Francesco asked the black student to repeat what he had said, and Grace translated it into Italian for him. "He said he saw you playing soccer, and he thought that you were pretty good with your feet." Francesco smiled and shook hands with new friend, calling out to him "Thank you," before leaving the school with Grace.

As they headed toward Grace's house, Francesco commented that the sky was not as blue as it was in Italy. It was rather orange-gray, darkened by the soot that fell like snow.

"These," said Grace, referring to the black flakes, "come from the valley where hundreds of furnaces are changing minerals into iron. It is their tall chimneys that give out all this filth. According to the experts, it is going to take at least twenty years of poverty and no productivity to return the air to its pristine quality."

"But how do you manage to live, breathing this poisoned air?" Francesco asked.

Grace shrugged her shoulders. "Oh, this happens only when the wind blows from west to east. You have to understand that these steel industries extend for one hundred miles, from Pittsburgh to Cleveland."

"Excuse me, how many kilometers are one hundred miles?"

"Oh, that is a good question," Grace frowned, "and I do not have an answer."

Francesco had been to both Pittsburgh and Cleveland, where his father had taken him to see some of his old compatriots. He remembered that from where he was now living, the two cities were in opposite directions; and it was at least an hour-and-a-half drive to either one. He concluded that it would take him three hours by car to go from one city to the other.

Then Francesco thought about the war, wanting once again to share his thoughts with her. It was evident that America was a strong nation and that what he was seeing was only a small part of the real United States. Stranger yet about the war was the fact that almost every family in Italy had some relatives in America, their second country.

"You are really different from the other young people of our age," Grace observed. "You have a style all of your own. Perhaps you suffered a lot during the war, but the war, at the same time, was a great teacher to you."

"Thanks for your comforting thoughts, but I want to tell you that I have thought of you a lot in the last twenty-four hours. I have to confess that we have a common denominator."

"Meaning…?"

"I, too, have suffered discrimination, and yet I feel free to reveal the most intimate things to you, because I regard you as my closest friend."

"I wanted you to know that, while they called you a wop and a fascist in this country, in Italy they used to call me 'the anti-fascist son of the American.' In fact, they told me some incredible stories to make me mad and to punish me, just because my father was in the United States."

"Can you tell me one?"

"Of course. A fascist friend called my father a traitor to my country, accusing him of being an American spy working in a steel mill where he made bombs to be used against us Italians. After those accusations, I did not want to be the son of an 'American' any longer. I wanted to be like all the young people, without the stigma of suspicion and with pride in being a fascist. As you see, we have had the same discrimination."

"How strange the world is!" Grace murmured.

By this time they had arrived at Grace's home. At the door stood a rather thin man in working clothes, with a black, dirty face and blue eyes like a clear sky threatened by the storm. Francesco was a bit uneasy, but as soon as Grace spoke to him, the tense atmosphere became pleasant. The man was her father, just returning from work. "Dad, I want you to meet a friend of mine."

"It is a pleasure," he said. " Come in, I want to wash my dirty hands."

"The pleasure is mine," answered the young man. "I am used to seeing my poor father coming home dirty every evening from a day of hard work."

Francesco became suddenly aware of the unmistakable aroma of bread just out of the oven. He had not smelled anything so good since leaving his neighborhood, where Giovanni the baker made the best bread in the world.

Grace called out to her mother. "Mama, come. I want you to meet my friend Francesco."

After an exchange of warm greetings, Grace's mother said, "Oh, what a pleasure to hear someone speak who has just arrived from beautiful Italy!"

"Madam, such a pleasure to hear you talk well of our country," Francesco replied politely.

"We would not feel any other way; the native country is never forgotten."

"What beautiful bread! It reminds me of Giovanni the baker's."

"You are very kind. Would you like to stay for a cup of coffee?"

"No, thanks, I will have to take a rain check. My father is waiting for me because we have been invited by my cousins for dinner."

As soon as Francesco left, Mrs. Ricchiuti wasted no time

in giving her opinion of her daughter's new friend. "He is different from other young people. He is not only polite, he is also well educated."

Her husband, Pasquale, was a bit more reserved in his judgment. "Before I give an opinion, I have to eat one hundred tons of pasta with him."

52

That evening at the dinner table, Francesco paid no attention to the conversation among the others. They were discussing preparations for making wine—the best place to buy grapes, the cleaning of the press—and these things did not interest him. Francesco had always complimented Angela on her culinary ability, but on this particular evening he spoke very little. His mind was elsewhere.

"You seem a bit worried," Iuccio observed. "Did something happen? Problems at school?"

Francesco seemed lost in thought before finally replying. "Surely, to start from zero—not knowing a word of English—is a real challenge. The school system is so different from ours, which educates only a small number of our youths. The school authorities are sensitive to what I have been experiencing and they go an extra mile for me. They have even provided me with an interpreter, a girl who is supposed to help me with my daily assignments. Their consideration at times seems almost excessive."

"I do not know if I misunderstood you," said Iuccio, "but did you say a girl interpreter?"

"Yes, a girl."

"What is her name?" asked Aunt Assunta.

"Grace."

"And her last name?"

"Ricchiuti."

"Where does she live?"

"Nearby."

Uncle Giosué commented that he worked with someone named Pasquale Ricchiuti. "If he is her father, then the girl must come from a good family."

"The family may be good, but she is American," Iuccio declared.

"What do you mean by that remark?" retorted Francesco.

"Nothing," he shrugged, "only that she is not Italian."

"You are absolutely wrong! She may be more Italian than you or I. She has been insulted by other Americans, called such things as 'wop'—just because she has an Italian name. And now, here you are calling her an American! She has been frustrated, humiliated, but she has never lost her pride as an Italian-American."

Iuccio was embarrassed. "What does 'wop' mean?" he asked sheepishly.

Francesco paused as if he were looking for the proper answer. He certainly didn't want to be in this situation, feeling uncomfortable, having to explain what 'wop' meant. Finally he said, "I asked my history teacher this same question. He told me that the original meaning is 'without papers.' But as time went by, the words took on a derogatory meaning. There are those who hold that the word is a corruption of the Spanish *guapo*, meaning to 'leave a good impression.' But it isn't clear how that could offend us."

Iuccio's comments about Grace had provoked a long silence around the dinner table. Francesco decided it was time to change the subject. "How are things going for Benjamin and Italo?" he ventured.

"They have written several times, and they seem to be optimistic about school. Benjamin is already thinking about a university," proud Angela responded.

It was getting late, and the evening drew to a close. Francesco and his father took the streetcar back to the house where they were renting a room from an old Calabrian couple who treated them like family.

That night Francesco did not sleep well, thinking about

the accelerated rhythm of life and starting to feel uneasy about the future. Without a doubt, Grace had become another reason for him to persevere. She was the most virtuous girl that he had ever met.

She was always positive with her comments, always patient as she taught him English, and always quick to encourage him by reminding him that many immigrants had started from scratch, but had seen the American Dream come true. She was cheerful, even when she spoke of unpleasant matters. He was also physically attracted to her, with her expressive emerald eyes, her sweet, inviting mouth, and her flowing, black hair, soft as velvet.

The sight of her delicate face had a calming effect on Francesco. The quiet joy he felt whenever he was with her was drawing him into something deeper than friendship. As more time passed, it began to seem as though their meeting had been predestined.

53 September of 1947 began in its usual marvelous way. The nip in the morning air coaxed the leaves into an array of brilliant colors, and the last of summer's flowers made their appearance in the garden. Francesco felt the urge to stop and rest among the cheerful chrysanthemums that filled the air with their fragrance. The days were still warm from the sun's rays filtering through puffs of clouds, while the chilly nights called for the season's first bedcovers.

That year the squirrels raced among the branches, partly to amuse themselves and partly to hunt for acorns. Older people claimed that this heightened activity among the squirrels, which led to larger stores of food, announced a long winter.

The most popular sport in the Ohio town where Francesco lived was football, which was always played from September to December. Every Friday evening under the lights of the stadium, everybody gathered to enjoy the game. Men, women, children, and the elderly attended with an almost religious devotion. Francesco went to the games, but always in the company of Grace. Because he didn't understand the game, he was puzzled that the players could be so violent at some times and so gentlemanly at others.

The stadium lights seemed almost blinding to Francesco, who had grown accustomed to complete darkness during the war. Fearing air raids, city dwellers and villagers alike were forced to shut their lights off at night and to make their way through narrow streets with lighted wooden sticks that looked like lightning bugs from far away.

One evening, just before the first football game of the season was to begin, a student sang "America, the Beautiful." Francesco, curious, asked Grace whether the song was the national anthem. She shook her head. "Usually all the games start with the national anthem, but our town is a real melting pot. Every year we come together to celebrate Immigrant's Day. 'America, the Beautiful' is the immigrant's hymn."

Toward the end of September, one day after school, Francesco and Grace went to the park next to the school instead of going home. It was enormous, as so many things appeared to be in this land. There were fields for soccer, baseball and football, tennis courts, a town swimming pool, and areas with benches and many, many trees. The autumn wind blew hard in parks like this one, causing thousands of leaves to fall into large piles where children liked to play, plunging into the leaves as if they were at the seashore, laughing and shouting.

As Grace and Francesco rested on a bench, they watched some young people playing soccer. The players were obviously immigrants because they were speaking languages other than English. Francesco was overcome by the desire to join them.

"Why don't you ask them when they will play next?" Grace suggested.

He shook his head. "No, I only want to enjoy your company now."

And so they just sat and enjoyed the sun and the breeze

that caressed them and stirred the leaves. The freshly cut grass made him think of hay-harvesting time in Italy.

"Do you have any photos of yourself?" asked Grace.

"Not as a small child, if that's what you mean. Unfortunately I left them all with my mother and sisters in Italy." This was not true. He simply was ashamed of showing her a photo of him in his big shoes, with the hundreds of nails shaped like mushrooms sticking out of them.

"What is your mother's name?" was Grace's next question.

"Maria."

"And your sisters' names?"

"The older, Dina; the younger, Lina."

"When you were a child, were you different from the serious and calm man that you seem to be now? Can you tell me of any mischievous episodes in your childhood?"

Francesco showed a smile, and confessed, "Those stories are a bit embarrassing. Still, I think I can tell you at least one. One Friday my sister Lina, with the passion of a young girl totally in love, made a fresh tomato pizza for her fiancé, who was supposed to arrive that evening after a hard day's work. That afternoon, a friend of mine and I came home from school and found a pizza just out of the oven. We ate it up in no time, without anyone disturbing us. In the evening, before the arrival of my future brother-in-law, my sister interrogated me and I told her that the cat had eaten the pizza. I guess she knew better. My sister's affection for me suddenly changed into a deadly poison, and her bites on my arms paralyzed me for some time. She made me pay for my sin—more than Adam and Eve paid for theirs! When her time comes, may she rest in peace. Her response was justified."

The sweetness of the night air drew them closer. Tenderly taking each other's hands, they began walking slowly toward the Ricchiuti home, from which drifted the aroma of scented espresso. The young people were becoming close. And Francesco was feeling more comfortable with the family. Their Italian origin, their dialect, and their traditions reinforced his attraction to them.

In Grace he saw the incentive for a career and the desire for a better future. Grace was his muse. On the other hand, she found comfort in Francesco's strong character, stable as a mountain and persevering. He was like Father Time, going forward in one direction, toward the future, knowing that sooner or later he would succeed in fulfilling his dreams.

She had observed his progress, fighting to learn a new language, working hard for a living, taking the dirtiest and lowest paying jobs. She liked his courage, optimism, and imagination. She used to say, "Man is judged in difficult situations." She was also happy to see that he was family-oriented. Every Saturday, Francesco and his father went to see Iuccio, spending the whole day with Angela and other relatives, relaxing with them.

54 On October 12, instead of going to the Italian festivities to commemorate Columbus Day, as millions of Italians still do, Francesco and Iuccio's family made wine to last for the entire year, as was customary in Italy. The aroma of must transported Francesco back to the times of vintage on his farm when, as a child, he would crush the grapes with his feet and drink the must from the tub.

October 31 arrived, and the air pinched one's cheeks on this night of Halloween, of ghosts and goblins. Children, dressed up in costumes, were the principal players, ready to frighten away any spirits eager to possess the living. Wearing scary masks representing witches and vampires, young and old invaded the streets of every American city, giving those who answered their door the ultimatum of a "trick or treat." In windows and on porches, lighted pumpkins with carved faces, some comical, others demonic, served to dissipate the malignant spirits and vampires.

This was the first Halloween Francesco had ever experienced, and he liked the atmosphere of excitement that exorcized fear of the dead. Grace asked Francesco to accompany her and her four-year-old niece, Patricia, as they went "trick-or-treating" around her neighborhood. Francesco dressed up like the devil; she, like a witch; and the little one, like a kitten with long whiskers.

Francesco told Grace that Halloween reminded him of carnival time in Italy when he, too, went around his village with friends, knocking on door after door. They would blacken their faces with a good rubbing of charcoal, and he would wear his father's old jacket upside down. Instead of "trick or treat," they would say, "Can we come in, the Masquerades?", and be rewarded with walnuts, almonds, and fruit.

Francesco told Grace about a book he had read called *The Toro Table*, which contained a vivid description of the Mardi Gras tradition. He eagerly described one of the most colorful aspects of the games. "And if, while these *saturnalia* (games) are going on, there is a marriage, two villagers wearing masks wait by the door of the church; and when the married couple exits, they grab the bride, who, though surprised, does not resist. They take her away under their arms and will not give her back until they get the silly gifts for which they asked. So, as you can see, even then, there existed a kind of 'trick or treat.'"

Then he asked her, "What does the word 'Halloween' mean?"

"Ah, of course, you could not possibly know it. It is a contraction of the name of a Catholic holiday called All Hallows Eve. The word 'hallows' means 'saints'; so, 'Halloween' means 'the eve of All the Saints.'"

The air was getting decidedly cool, rendering her rosy cheeks more beautiful. He had never desired her more than at that moment. After a short pause, he spoke in a serious tone. "I do not have the resources to buy you an engagement ring, but I would like you to promise me that one day you will be mine."

She was surprised by the unexpected request—in fact, speechless—yet those words made her heart feel good. She had had that same dream, but it had seemed too far away for her. She looked at him for a while and then, with much tenderness, she answered him with a prolonged kiss.

Little Patricia was getting tired and wanted to go home when suddenly Francesco became aware of the noise of birds. What he heard was a roar that was getting louder and louder. "What is happening?" said he, somewhat annoyed at the disturbance.

"Oh, those are geese coming in from Canada. They are big birds that leave cold places to go to a warm climate, like the swallows in Italy at the end of the summer."

"Ah, yes, I have something in common with them."

"Meaning what?" she said.

"Migration, hunger," he responded.

The number of trick-or-treaters was diminishing, so the three of them started heading home too. On the way, they accidentally touched some wires that had been strung up between two trees and, much to their surprise, were instantly doused with water. Some rascals had apparently balanced a container of water very precariously on the wires, hoping that some innocent victims would come along and unwittingly dislodge it. Francesco, Grace, and Patricia took the container home and were delighted to see that this wet trick would produce a treat, for the container contained candy, chocolates, and even some money amounting to two dollars and fifty cents.

Iuccio did not approve of this American masquerading tradition of trick or treat, because it was so close to the celebration of "All Saints and Souls Day," a time when people in Italy would get ready spiritually to honor their martyrs and dead ones by placing white, yellow, and orange chrysanthemums on the graves.

"Several times I have told you that the Americans are wild people," Iuccio began.

Francesco stopped him immediately. "You have to understand that this country has only been around for two hundred years. Their monuments smell of fresh cement, and their traditions are new. Even a blind man would recognize these differences. One cannot look at such a new country with an old mentality."

But Iuccio was not listening. His disillusionment with America was increasing and making him more dissatisfied. His unhappiness was like an avalanche of snow, which begins with a rustle and ends with thunder. He was no longer the egocentric and ambitious exhibitionist who had been so sure of himself at one time. He had become a disenchanted cynic, a broken and morose man who saw his future only as one of uncertainty.

55 Several weeks before Christmas, Francesco's mother, Maria, arrived from Italy. Never before had she ventured outside her village's walls, but with enthusiasm she had gathered enough energy to face the long journey to America, thus fulfilling the dream of being reunited as a family after many years of separation—first from her husband, mostly because of the war, and more recently from her son.

Her husband, Joseph, had received her letters from Italy during his fourteen years in America; but because Maria had had someone else write them for her, he always had to read between the lines to understand how much she missed him and what a great vacuum his departure had created. This illiterate woman had been the heart and the mind of their home and the source of much energy for the whole family.

Here in Ohio a gift from Joseph was awaiting her—a house that he had bought after years of sacrifice. Father and son cleaned and painted their modest new home, readying it to welcome her and make her happy.

A few days after Mrs. Salvato's arrival, she and her family celebrated Thanksgiving with the Ceppones. Assunta had prepared a turkey, a symbol of this day of grace dating back to the time of the first pilgrims.

Before everybody sat down to eat, and before giving the invocation, Assunta asked that everyone join hands in a circle and bow their head as a sign of reverence, while she pronounced the following words: "We thank the Lord for this great joy of being together for the first time after so much suffering—united as before, hoping never to be separated again—and for the abundance of everything in this blessed land. In the name of the Father, of the Son, and of the Holy Ghost."

After dinner, despite the inclement weather, the annual parade took place as scheduled, in spectacular fashion and as amusing as always. Coincidentally, the predominant colors were those of the Italian flag: red, symbol of blood and passion; green, symbol of growth and life; and white, symbol of purity. The parade featured gigantic plastic balloons, bigger-than-life replicas of Santa Claus and a turkey. There were bands led by majorettes, and floats with different themes, like Alice in Wonderland, and, at the very end, Santa's sleigh and the red-nosed reindeer. To the delight of shouting children and the applauding crowd, an enormous evergreen tree at the center of the town square was lighted. The little band of recent immigrants was impressed without really understanding the purpose of the ceremony.

At that time the Italian newspaper *Progresso* was promoting a concert called "the show of the century," praising the voice of an Italian-American singer by the name of Sergio Franchi. His pictures decorated the shops of many neighboring cities, underscoring the passion for Italian folk music. So, early on December 15, the Tottis and Francesco got into the car of Dominic Mazzarino, a friend of the Ceppone family, and drove toward the outskirts of Pittsburgh, the Steel City, to the Palace Theater, where they had the good luck to get seats in the first row. The singer turned out to be exceptionally talented. In fact, at the end of the first half of his performance, the public was so appreciative that they applauded him for ten minutes.

During the intermission, Francesco went to the lavatory, where he overheard many Italian dialects. Suddenly he heard an angry voice, saying, "Damn you, stupid."

Recognizing the unmistakable dialect of his village, Francesco approached the two young men who were arguing and said, "Ah, the most beautiful music in the world—my native dialect!"

"What music?" one of them answered sarcastically. "I'm just yelling at my 'blind' brother for urinating on my shoes!"

"That is holy water," retorted the other, laughing.

"For me, this is divine music that can only come from one place—my village," Francesco said. The three looked at each other for an instant before the older of the two brothers asked, "Who are you?"

"I am Maria Salvato's son. I used to live on Barbacano Street."

"Oh, my goodness," the younger brother said. "Now I recognize you. You were a child when I left Italy in 1939. I'm Luigi Francala."

They immediately embraced, and Luigi introduced him to his older brother, Nuccio, who had arrived in America in 1934. They exchanged addresses and telephone numbers. Francesco then took the two brothers to meet Iuccio, Benjamin, Italo, and Dominic, all of whom were waiting for him in the foyer.

Iuccio recognized Luigi at once. A few months before departing for America in 1939, the young man had won a ten-kilometer race, competing against one hundred other boys in Campobasso. "I remember you very well!" Iuccio told him. "You are the only one from our village to have honored us in the past."

Before returning to their seats, they promised to meet when the program ended. The performance was concluded with a selection of Neapolitan classical songs and the beautiful aria "*Va Pensiero.*" The jubilant audience went crazy with joy, begging for encore after encore.

After finding one another afterwards among the huge crowd, Dominic, who was worried about the long drive home, declined the warm invitation of the Francala brothers to join them for a glass of wine. But he promised that the five of them would come for a visit on a weekend in the near future. After a brotherly embrace, they separated in the parking lot.

56 Christmas Day was fast approaching and the school was in a festive mood, playing music that sounded like the ringing of church bells, music that crossed all barriers and cultures. Students in every classroom were singing Christmas songs, imitating Bing Crosby and two Italian-Americans, Perry Como and Frank Sinatra, popular singers of the era. Next to the principal's office there was a beautiful Christmas tree decorated with many ornaments and a simple nativity scene enhanced by a string of twinkling lights.

One day after school Francesco spotted his history teacher and wanted to ask him a question. Mr. Conti invited him into the teachers' room. There he found Mr. Nolfi and Mr. Zarrella, the English and Latin teachers. He was a bit embarrassed by the presence of the two other teachers, but the atmosphere quickly became cordial and he soon felt comfortable. How strange! thought Francesco. In America teachers were willing to communicate with him as equals. They seemed to be down to earth, while in Italy they lived on Mount Olympus.

"Tell me," said Mr. Conti, "how did the trip to Pittsburgh go?"

"It is a beautiful city and I had a great time," answered Francesco, "even though it was cold and there was snow everywhere." After talking about how Sergio Franchi had not disappointed the public, he recounted the remarkable story of his encounter with fellow townsmen.

Mr. Zarrella was nodding his head. "These things are very possible. There are many Italians who work in the big steel industries in that area."

"I agree," said Mr. Conti. "From 1901 to 1941 almost six million Italians arrived and most of them are now living in the large American cities of the East, such as Boston, New York, Philadelphia, Pittsburgh, and Cleveland."

Francesco found the courage to ask a bold question, one

that had been bothering him for some time. "If there are so many Italians in this land, why is it that I do not see one Italian name in the history books? Are they not also Americans?"

Mr. Conti began leafing through a book and smiled when he found the quote he was looking for. He quickly paraphrased the words of Nicholas Murray Butler, president of Columbia University in New York: "Italy's place in civilization is best shown by trying to subtract that place from world history…. Take away her scientific accomplishments, her statesmanship, her leadership of the world for many years, and what do you have left? The world is decapitated…. You can subtract Italian cultures from civilization only by destroying that civilization."

Francesco was so spellbound that he interrupted. "Excuse me, Mr. Conti, why isn't what you just read in history books?"

"Because," replied Mr. Conti, "America is a great nation, but it incubates great injustices. You have to understand that those who write textbooks do so from their own point of view. I wonder whether, for example, writers will address the contribution of native Americans who volunteered to defend the United States against the Japanese. Will there be mention made of their heroism in the Pacific during the Second World War? The use of their Navajo language as a code kept the Japanese in the dark."

Francesco was stunned. The teacher's observations, in their educated objectivity, were even more persuasive than Grace's passionate description of bigotry. The cruel truth of discrimination in his adopted land floored him for the second time, but he was ready to delve deeper. "What is the source of this discrimination? Who is this invisible enemy that we face?"

The three teachers smiled at each other. And then the Latin teacher said, "Naturally, *inter nos* (between us), they are descendants of those people who came here from several countries of northern Europe."

"Could you give me an example of discrimination against us?" asked their inquisitive student.

"Certainly," replied Mr. Conti. "Take, Italy, for example. Its recent, glorious past is not well represented in the American history books. So when one speaks of Christopher Columbus, it is Spain that comes to mind. The names Giovanni and Sebastiano Caboto, from Genoa, become John and Sebastian Cabot and are identified as English explorers in history books. Giovanni Verrazzano discovered the Hudson Bay years before the arrival of Henry Hudson, from whom it took its name.

"There is no mention in the books that one of the most important phrases of the Declaration of Independence, 'All men are by nature equally free and independent,' was inspired by a Florentine physician named Phillip Mazzei.

"In no school text will you find that during the American Civil War two regiments were recruited among Italians. The Garibaldi Guards, which fought in Lincoln's army against the separatists of the South, comprised one. Nor will you find that the first band of the famous United States Marines had been recruited in Italy by Thomas Jefferson, one of the founding fathers of this country, who also happened to be a passionate italophile.

"In the Philadelphia Art Museum, there is a beautiful necklace called Glass Beads, made in Jamestown, Virginia, between 1621 and 1625, testimony to sixteen Venetians who had established the first glass factory there."

Noticing that Francesco's interest was far from flagging, Mr. Conti continued on. "In 1635 an Italian named Peter Caesar Alberti began a tobacco plantation in New Amsterdam, which is now New York State. Some people from Piemonte, Italy, introduced the silk industry in Georgia, and in 1657 another three hundred Italians arrived in Delaware for the same reason.

"In the mid-nineteenth century Paolo Busti, from Milan, as a representative of the Holland Land Company, developed three million acres of land in the states of New York and Pennsylvania and started villages that became cities. Buffalo is just one example.

"But to complete this industrial, cultural, and scientific mosaic were the great Italian architects, painters, sculptors, scientists, and educators. In our magnificent capital of Washington D.C., there is little that is not Italian, from the Brunelleschi dome of Capitol Hill and the Lincoln Memorial sculptured by the Piccirilli brothers, to the frescos of Costantino Brumidi, called the Michelangelo of the United States, who came to Washington from Italy in 1852. That same year he distinguished himself with his marvelous 4,664-square-foot frescos of patriotic and allegorical figures of the giants of the democracy. Among them were Benjamin Franklin, Thomas Jefferson, John Hancock, Henry Clay, Andrew Jackson, Horatio Gates, Alexander Hamilton, Roger Sherman, and Robert Morris. Among this historical artistry are depictions of the landing of Christopher Columbus, the arrival of the Pilgrims, George Washington at Valley Forge, the Boston Massacre, and William Penn making peace with the Indians.

"Brumidi worked on the beautification of the Capitol for the last twenty-five years of his life. He died several months after a freak accident in which he was left suspended from the scaffolding, but saved himself by hanging on with his right hand. At the time of his death in 1880, he had finished all but one of his frescos.

"Four days after his death, Senator Woorhees, of Indiana, immortalized him with these words: 'It matters little, however, whether we, or those who come after us, do anything to perpetuate his memory. The walls of this Capitol will hold his fame fresh and ever-increasing as long as they themselves shall stand.'

"Many other Italians contributed to the grandeur of the Capitol, making it the most beautiful architectural jewel of this city named for the first president of the United States. Among them are names like Capellano, Cardelli, Causici, Cerere, Ciani, Iardella, Valaperti, Vincenti, and scores more.

"And Italians have participated in all wars, from the War of Independence in 1776 to the Civil War of 1860 and then to all those of the 1900s."

The teacher stopped, thinking that Francesco had enough

information for one day, but the rapt expression on the young man's face induced Mr. Nolfi, the English teacher, to continue. "There are those who attack us openly. For example, the anglophile writer Madison Grant, author of *The Passing of the Great Race*, clearly stated that persons from northern Europe were superior to those from the Mediterranean and Balkan nations...."

"But why are they hostile toward us poor immigrants?" Francesco asked angrily, thinking that being born in another part of the world should not constitute a crime.

Mr. Conti thought for a while before continuing. "There are various reasons for this discrimination, and I will mention only three of them—the economy, ignorance, and prejudice. The country's first strong economy emerged during and after the Revolution of 1776 and continued to grow, thanks to the free contribution of the black slaves. The industrialists maintained the status quo until 1900, when black manpower was replaced by an even hungrier group—immigrants. When these immigrants were no longer satisfied with their low-paying dirty jobs, they rebelled, just as the Negroes with Nat Turner had done before them. The only difference was that the blacks fought to free themselves from the chains of slavery, while the new immigrants were looking for economic freedom."

The teacher, though a bit tired, wanted Francesco to receive the full impact of his message, so he pressed on: "With his book *Bitter Cry of the Children,* the writer John Spargo sensitized the hardest hearts of America to the inhumane work conditions in the mines of Pennsylvania and of West Virginia during the early part of the 1900s, especially those conditions under which more than one million children worked twelve hours a day. Bent over the troughs, young boys sat for hours, extracting pieces of slate or other impurities from the coal as it was expelled from the washing tubs, so that most of them became deformed and hunched-over like old people.

"As for the workers, the most effective way for them to earn respect was through the strikes promoted by John Mitchell and other union representatives of coal mines.

"So, you can see, Francesco," concluded Mr. Conti, "that by promoting the notion of inferior ethnic groups, a few were able to exploit the many for economic gains. Ignorance did the rest, as well as the prejudice of those who failed to understand that the greatness of this country lies in the energy brought by new arrivals and instead viewed their presence as an economic threat. Often the bias comes from former immigrants who are tired of doing the dirtiest low-paying jobs."

Time had passed quickly during Francesco's visit with his teachers. He had learned a great deal and cordially bid the teachers goodbye. He started to walk toward home, continuing to reflect on the contradictions of a nation that took pride in welcoming millions of oppressed immigrants and filling their hearts with words like "give me the hungry, the needy" yet showing in deeds its cruel face. It was like a struggle between Good and Evil, God and the Prince of Darkness, the god of reason and the devil of violence and persecution.

When Francesco returned to school the next day, he told Mr. Conti about the growing doubts in his heart about the country he now lived in. His teacher was also a good psychologist. He knew that what he had told Francesco the day before had touched a nerve. Now he wanted to assure his student that it was necessary to know history so that one could see better into the future, to use history as a source of energy and not to feel threatened by it. Also, he wanted to encourage Francesco to look objectively at all the facts. "For example," Mr. Conti said, "the Founding Fathers exhausted much of their energy debating passionately about liberty and the prosperity of the future generations. They were men who could not tolerate the burden of injustice or the abuses of power. They wanted to protect future generations from bigotry." He was hoping that these kinds of facts would arouse Francesco's curiosity and feelings of affection for this generous land.

But Francesco was wondering how it was possible that some of these Founding Fathers had had slaves. How could one defend his rights while chained? Wasn't slavery perpetuated when children were exploited in the coal mines, or even now when millions of immigrants are kept in the most humiliating jobs? It was up to immigrants like himself, perhaps, to burn away these impurities.

Mr. Conti patted him on the back. "You will see," he said gently, "America the Great will, in the end, justly reward the Italians who have reached enviable levels in all fields, in spite of the ostracism, neglect, and lynchings they have endured. Despite its injustices, America is still a country to admire, the one described by Lincoln in his Gettysburg Address as a 'government of the people, by the people, for the people.'"

57 The Sunday before Christmas, Assunta and her newly arrived sister-in law, Maria, talked about being together on Christmas Eve. For such an occasion, Assunta had in mind serving a traditional menu. "Dear sister-in law," said Assunta, "with your help we will make the seven fishes."

"Why seven?" asked the newcomer.

"Because it is an Italian-American tradition," she answered. "We make seven different kinds of fish."

"But will we be able to find them?" For Maria it seemed impossible to find such a variety of food, because in the last ten years, especially during wartime and immediately afterwards, she could only hope to buy eel in Italy.

"Certainly," answered her sister-in law. "We could even buy more, but our tradition calls for only seven fishes, even though this custom is not well known in Italy. We will need anchovies to put in our hand-made spaghetti, and then the six others: clams, lobsters, eel, squid, codfish, and mullet."

Maria smiled and nodded. "Ah, a supper conceived with the affection of a true sister! I will be happy to do my part to make it an unforgettable evening."

When a car horn sounded from the street, they rushed out to the porch, and there was the friendly godfather, Dr. Alfredo Santillo, from New York. He wanted to make a surprise visit before the holidays. His Cadillac in front of the house seemed as long as a train. Out of it emerged his wife, Isabella; his mother, Mrs. Rosina; and two young fellows, sixteen-year-old Alfred and fourteen-year-old Joseph. It was a happy moment. Everyone embraced, especially the elderly women, who had been childhood friends.

While Angela and Assunta were preparing lunch, Maria and Mrs. Rosina sat on the sofa in the living room, satisfying their hearts with childhood memories. The young people went out to admire the huge car and to sample its comforts, and soon they started playing in the snow. Iuccio and Dr. Santillo joined the others at the table. They opened a bottle of homemade, fizzy wine specially prepared for the holidays, and Giosué, the man of the house, immediately began to fill the glasses. Iuccio raised his in a toast—"Cheers and may it bring us health."

"But also joy," the good physician answered, touching the glasses of Giosué, Uncle Joseph, Francesco, and then Iuccio. "How are things going for all of you?"

Iuccio was quick to answer. "To tell you the truth, I am a bit disappointed. Not for my children, but for me, because I cannot find a job. In fact, I am contemplating returning to Italy. Here, life is a jungle where I do not feel secure."

"Dear Iuccio, you will be making the biggest mistake if you decide to go back. I am surprised that a man like you, such a veteran of difficult storms, is afraid of a little heat. This beautiful cow, America, is easily milked. It is only a matter of time."

"But I am fed up looking for a job and living within four walls."

Angela was cooking, but she was listening attentively to the conversation, hoping that the doctor would be able to convince her husband that work could be found.

"My dear friend," Dr. Santillo said in a strong voice, "this country has been synonymous with the land of opportunity since the arrival of the pioneers, while in our village we were still victimized by servitude. For example, in our South we worked for peanuts for the local lords and then we would take them a rooster on New Year's Eve to show them our gratitude! Do you remember when our ancestors had to be satisfied with working for one fourth of the harvested crop, the rest going to the owner? Here, you don't have to thank anybody except God for giving you health."

Hearing these old stories always upset Iuccio and made him defensive. "In Italy I was not a pauper and I did not pick crops. I had a steady job there, which was protected by the government. The labor laws in this country are some of the most antiquated of the civilized world. They protect the employers, instead of the unfortunate souls who are breathing gases underground in the coal mines. Here, one has to have all kinds of insurance to protect his family—hospital, fire, car, life. All of these are burdens on you."

"I didn't say that this country is perfect," the physician countered, though he appeared to be affected by Iuccio's words. "There are injustices now, and there will always be. But America also offers many possibilities, and through hard work you can reach the stars. You have to understand, even if things happen a bit too slowly for you, they will change for the better. Haven't they demolished the shameful slavery at the cost of a civil war? It has only been two hundred years since the thirteen colonies rebelled against the King of England. But the principle of 'no taxation without representation' still remains. Our human rights are safeguarded by the Constitution, which gives us freedom of the press, of speech, and religion. Here, not even the President is above the law."

"Excuse me, Doctor," interjected Joseph, Francesco's father, "but has this 'Constitution' always existed?"

"Certainly. For almost two hundred years."

"But then, even the Constitution is discriminatory," Joseph reasoned. "I, like so many other Italians, were given the worst jobs just because my name ended in a vowel."

"You are absolutely right, dear Uncle Joseph. That happened before the war, but now with labor unions protecting you, it is no longer possible."

Giosué lifted his glass of wine. "Doctor, I propose a toast to your health, to ours, to the Constitution that protects our rights, and to that logical, wise, and pragmatic capitalistic system that brings us economic success. The question of the purity or the impurity of one's blood or nobility doesn't exist here, as in other parts of the world. Nor does the code of inequality. In this country all children and young people are obliged to go to school, while in Italy the poor people are expected to go to work after the fifth grade."

"To our health," Dr. Alfredo said, dropping the subject at this point.

In the background the air was filled with the melody of Christmas songs by Perry Como, the famous barber turned singer. Angela called to the young people playing outside and announced to everyone that lunch was ready. As soon as everyone was seated at the table, Italo, the youngest, said in a hurry, "Good appetite," as if he wanted to lighten the mood. But the good grandmother quickly removed the fork from his hand. As she had done on Thanksgiving Day, she asked all to unite for a small prayer. "We ask You, Almighty God, to protect us all, especially our dear guests in their long trip back home, and to bless our food on the table."

"Amen," responded several voices.

"Good appetite to all," Italo added, "and enough with your arguing."

But later in the evening it appeared likely that the dispute would resume when Iuccio said, "Godfather Alfredo, I hope that I am wrong, but it seems that we were better off when times were worse."

The doctor's response was unexpected. "Come to New York with me. There are endless possibilities of finding work in the big cities, where dreams are more likely to come true than in the smaller towns."

JANUS

58 Like many other immigrants, Francesco was amazed by the holiday activities in school on the last day before Christmas vacation. In every class, students, especially female, exchanged gifts as people do in Italy on January 6, the day of the Epiphany. At first Francesco thought he might have misunderstood some announcement. Perhaps he, too, should have participated in bringing some gifts, but then he saw that there were many boys with empty hands.

About eleven o'clock Francesco heard some voices in the corridors, followed by an announcement over the loudspeaker inviting all the students to the theater. The seniors were called first, then juniors, and finally sophomores. Contrary to all the other assembles, there was total silence when they all sat down. Suddenly the lights went off and a melodious chorus of "Joy to the World" was heard.

A line of girls entered from the right, illuminating the auditorium with candles. They wore green skirts and red handkerchiefs on white blouses. The boys, wearing dark suits with white shirts and red ties, formed another line entering from the left. As they marched toward the stage, they sang several Christmas songs. Everyone rose and remained standing for the last song, the "Allelujah Chorus" from Handel's *Messiah*, which was followed by continuous and tumultuous applause and cries of "Bravo."

Francesco enjoyed the show tremendously, especially the "Allelujah," which he had never heard before. Despite the large crowd greeting and embracing each other, Francesco succeeded in finding Grace, who was waiting for him next to her locker. He was still curious about the day's events, and as they walked toward her home, he confessed, "I still do not understand this celebration, even though I really enjoyed it."

As soon as they arrived home, Mrs. Ricchiuti prepared coffee and some freshly baked goodies. Her smiling face reflected a happiness that was matched only by her singing, which at times could be heard out in the street.

"Where will you spend Christmas Eve?" she asked Francesco with obvious interest.

"Mother," cautioned Grace, "that is an indiscreet question."

"Not at all," Francesco said quickly. "I will tell you. We will go to the home of Uncle and Aunt Ceppone, who have also invited Grace for that evening. They are all anxious to meet her."

Mrs. Ricchiuti regarded Francesco warmly. "For me, she can do as she pleases, but it would be better to talk it over with her father."

The day before Christmas, the three musketeers, as Francesco, Benjamin and Italo called themselves, met downtown and together walked up and down the main street with their eyes fixed on the store windows filled with winter wonders. They noticed that there were many Santas ringing their bells loudly in front of the stores, trying to raise funds for the poor.

Early in the afternoon, the Salvatos took the bus to Youngstown to meet the Ceppones for a day of shopping. When they entered the Rullis' store, which specialized in Italian merchandise, Maria immediately basked in the aroma of the things she loved: Parma hams and cheeses, provolone, cod and many other types of fish.

Francesco returned home a little late from the city, showered quickly, and headed to the Ricchiutis', where little Patricia was the first to welcome him. She begged him to play games with her.

"Look what Santa has brought you," Francesco said, presenting her with a beautiful doll. Then he greeted everyone, shaking hands first with Tony and Lucy, Grace's brother- and sister-in-law. The whole family showed appreciation for the beautiful gift Francesco had bought that afternoon.

"Will you stay with us?" Tony asked.

"It would be a real pleasure, but I have promised to go to my cousins'. When Grace is ready, we will have to be on our way."

A few minutes later, Grace and Francesco left, arriving at the Ceppones' just in time to eat. Everyone had been waiting anxiously. "Why so late?" asked Iuccio.

"The bus schedule for the holidays is different, and we had to wait longer than usual. I want you to meet Grace." All welcomed her as part of the family, and she immediately felt at home.

"It is a real pleasure to meet all of you," Grace said pleasantly. "Francesco has told me so much about you that I can recognize each of you."

The house had a special aroma, and between Perry Como's music and the laughter, joy seemed to reign. Everyone took a seat, reserving the head of the table for the special guest. But Grace felt ill at ease about being the center of attention and begged Francesco to take the place of honor while she sat next to him.

All enjoyed the delicious variety of food, one dish after another, complimenting not only Assunta but also Maria, who had lent a helping hand.

Iuccio's usual antagonistic remarks toward his mother-in-law had not let up over time. "I would have preferred a codfish from Termoli," he complained sarcastically, as if determined to spoil the beautiful dinner.

"And what do you mean by that wisecrack?" Assunta demanded in return.

"I am saying that one can't find fresh fish here. People don't know how to eat here."

"What do you know?" responded Angela. "Frozen fish, cooked with all the affection of a mother, is better than any fresh fish."

Benjamin, trying to change the subject, suggested to Francesco that afterwards they go to a fabulous restaurant in town that featured good food, an orchestra and singers, and dancing that would most likely go on until morning.

Maria was shocked at Benjamin's idea. For her, Christmastime was only about going to church and being home with family by the fireplace, telling stories or reciting poetry about Baby Jesus.

Benjamin was amused by her ingenuousness. "Aunt Maria, your observations are correct up to a certain point. This country was founded on Christian religious principles, but not all Christians celebrate Christmas the way we do. And not everyone is a Christian. There are also people of other faiths."

"Which ones?" asked Maria.

"So many," he responded. "Jews, Buddhists, Moslems, Hindus, to name some. We live in a democracy here, which means, above all, that there is respect for religions."

This news sounded quite bizarre to Mrs. Salvato, who made the Sign of the Cross, finding comfort only in her God and her Church.

Midnight was fast approaching. This would be the right time to depart before a real argument could take place. Francesco and Grace stood up and announced their departure.

"Where are you going?" protested Iuccio. "This is card-playing time."

"The last bus departs at twelve o'clock, and we have to take it," Grace said gently. Iuccio's response was to take the cards and throw them into the air, showering some on the guests.

The Salvatos and Grace embraced everyone before leaving. Grace was visibly shaken by Iuccio's tempestuous behavior. While on the bus, Francesco tried to explain that Iuccio had a double personality. What she had observed was his negative side, the bossy one. But when he was in good humor, he could be very pleasant and charming.

"I believe you, but I have to tell you that I have never seen such a scandalous scene like tonight," Grace answered, a little coldly. But then he took her hand, as if to warm it up, and guided it to the small box he was holding.

"What is it?" she asked.

"It is past twelve. Merry Christmas," he responded.

She gently opened the box to find a gold pin in the form of a lily. "How beautiful!" she exclaimed. "It is my favorite flower. How did you know that I liked lilies?"

"I saw the way you admired them in your backyard."

"But I do not have anything for you."

"You already have given me what I want," he responded.

"Meaning?"

"My happiness is due only to you."

They were sitting behind Mr. and Mrs. Salvato, so Grace whispered, "Merry Christmas," before kissing him. When the bus stopped by Grace's house, she wished the Salvatos a *"Buon Natale"* and kissed them on both cheeks. The night air was cold. As the parents started in the direction of their own home, Francesco and Grace remained locked in an embrace. After a prolonged kiss, she closed her door and he went home.

59 Despite the minor incident at Iuccio's house, this Christmas season had been a happy time, markedly different from those during the war. However, the biggest surprise for Francesco was the ferocity of a snowstorm on New Year's Day.

It came like a polar bear with a hardened heart. It paralyzed one fourth of the United States, the whole northeast part of the country. Of course, the squirrels had already signaled the approaching storm with their frenzied pursuit of acorns in the preceding months. It seemed that the aged Italian man at the fall parade had been right about the squirrels. But the extent of the storm was the surprise.

Nature had whitened everything with two feet of snow, and traffic came to a halt. The wave of bad weather and severe temperatures damaged the electric and telephone lines, leaving half a million people in the dark. Fortunately, Francesco's area had electricity, and he received news by radio. The governor declared a state of emergency, calling out the National Guard to clear the principal arteries of the big cities, especially those leading to hospitals.

Francesco put on his father's boots and, armed with a shovel, removed a "mountain of snow" around his house. Then he made a path to Grace's house just a few doors away, where he removed some more snow. He was hardly inside the house when Mrs. Ricchiuti offered him a cup of coffee to warm him up.

"How comfortable these homes are—so warm," declared Francesco, sitting with the family at the round table in the kitchen.

"Almost all the American houses have this heating system," Grace said.

Grace's father, who worked in the coal mines, explained: "Ohio and Pennsylvania have enough coal to heat the whole world forever. As a matter of fact, there are some abandoned coal mines in Pennsylvania that have been burning for decades, and nobody has ever been able to extinguish them. Summer or winter, smoke continues to come out of those mines."

Francesco immediately thought about the cold winters in his native land and commented, "It is difficult to explain this divine injustice. Some have so much and others have nothing. During the war, if we needed to warm up, we had to go to the blacksmith's shop or an olive crusher's shop, or the shop of some cobbler who always had a brazier on."

"I want you to know that during my childhood we did the same thing," Mr. Ricchiuti said. "When they kicked us out of one shop, we went to another to warm up. We never had enough firewood in our homes."

The two were quiet for a moment, as if they were reliving these experiences, which in their similarity, seemed to bring them closer. Grace took advantage of the pause to join in the conversation. "This weather has spoiled the New Year's festivities."

"Too bad," commented Francesco. "I was looking forward to seeing how Americans celebrate New Year's Eve."

"How do you celebrate it in Italy?" Grace asked.

"Well, we have to be careful as to which Italy we are talking about," Francesco began. "The rich celebrate it in the big hotels or in private clubs, wearing tuxedos and long gowns, while the poor gather at someone's house in the neighborhood to eat lentils and other peasant food."

Grace's mother started laughing because she knew that her daughter would not have any idea what a peasant's dinner would be like.

"Is it true that on New Year's Eve Americans get dressed up for an evening of dancing and pleasure?" Francesco asked.

Mr. Ricchiuti nodded. "Yes, it is true, but it is also true that many people go to work on New Year's Eve. Factories are closed only on Christmas Day or for severe, inclement weather like today."

It started to snow again, slowly, without the fury of the last twenty-four hours. Francesco and Grace went out to enjoy the beauties of nature and to chat with neighbors who were all busy removing snow from around their homes and yards. Many mothers came out to pull their children on small sleighs. The children, looking like miniature stuffed Santas, seemed intrigued by the winter phenomenon. Meanwhile, the bigger children, with occasional shouts of "Happy New Year," were having a good time making a snowman and throwing snowballs.

60 Iuccio continued to live for his children, but he also seemed determined to control their destiny. While Benjamin continued to heed his father's advice to follow his monsignor uncle's footsteps, Italo was being a bit rebellious. Perhaps he had inherited that trait from his father, or perhaps it was due to the accident to his hand from the threshing machine. Whatever the reason, his parents secretly cared more for Benjamin, who seemed to be a model young man. During the Christmas vacation, he got up early every morning to go to church, a habit surely acquired from the Salesian Fathers in Italy and also from his religious uncle in Penne. He had continued the practice in New Rochelle at the Salesian school.

To maintain their children in private schools was very expensive. Iuccio had not found a job yet, and what Angela earned was not adequate. Against their will, they enrolled the two boys in a local public high school, as Francesco had done.

During the first months of 1949, the school authorities published the names of the highest achieving students. Among them was that of Benjamin, who had attained the highest grades and also obtained the honor of student editor of the school paper, *The Iron Star*, so called for the many steel factories in that long, wide valley between Pittsburgh and Cleveland. Benjamin had also been nominated to be president of the student council, a position that would entitle him to defend the students' rights.

He also accepted the role of the young Frank Sinatra in one of the school plays. He made the girls go crazy, so perfect was his vocal impersonation. He was becoming the most popular student in the school, and his counselors told him that if he continued to get good grades, he would receive many scholarships and awards at the end of the school year.

Iuccio looked at Benjamin's accomplishments with ambivalence. On one hand, he was excited because he could never have imagined that either boy would have achieved so much in two years. On the other hand, Benjamin's success was diverting him from the religious path recommended by his uncle and his father and, indirectly, by his entire family, who had praised him to all their fellow townsmen for his sanctity. Furthermore, his father was not pleased that Benjamin was going out with different girls after school, spending too much time with them, and coming home late at night.

This change became another reason for Iuccio to quarrel with his wife and his mother-in-law, who insisted that Benjamin's behavior with girls was normal in this culture as was going to the school dances on Friday evenings after a football game.

Iuccio, who understood the danger better than the rest, confessed to Francesco that the change in his son worried him. Francesco was used to being the shock absorber between both sides. To calm him down, Francesco told him that he was overreacting. "Tell me, Iuccio, don't you remember how mischievous you were at our age?" Iuccio managed a half-smile.

In truth, Francesco had noticed a change in his young cousin. But he attributed it directly to the rigid education at the seminary. He remembered also that, in the name of certain principles, Benjamin had even rejected the caresses of the Albano sisters during the cold winter nights spent together in Campobasso. To Francesco, it seemed logical that this kind of action—striving to be a model student—would eventually have a reaction, and that feelings, long repressed, would finally be freed.

Francesco remembered a barbaric episode in which one seven-year-old friend had been forced by his father to swim naked across the Tappino River and back on an icy winter day. This was the father's attempt to teach the boy to obey him. After that, the little fellow became a model of piety. Who knows what became of him once freed from the father's control!

Iuccio could not resort to such extreme discipline. Thinking that the American ways were changing his children, all he could say was, "Damn America." One thing was certain, though: the American ways were very good and healthy for Benjamin. They gave him hope that one day he, too, would find his El Dorado. He was a satisfied, happy boy, finally feeling free from the heavy burden of past restrictions.

61 In June of 1949, a monk named Father Pasquale arrived from Italy as a guest of Francesco, who immediately took him for a walk around his neighborhood. At one point, they came to the spectacular cathedral of Saint Patrick. The Franciscan monk, intrigued by its beauty, wanted to see it. Knowing that it was close to Francesco's house and assuming that it served as his parish, he began thinking that it might be possible to celebrate Mass there the next day.

In the church's well-furnished office, Monsignor Kenney

sccmcd at first very proud to show them the inside of the church. But when the monk expressed the desire to celebrate Mass there next morning, the monsignor refused indignantly, telling him that the parish was attended exclusively by Irish people and suggesting that he and Francesco go to an Italian parish.

The two guests were dumbstruck by that answer. Nevertheless, they decided to pay a visit to Father Palermo at the small Italian church, which looked more like a hut than a godly place. Father Palermo appeared to be leaving just as they arrived.

"Good morning, Father," said Francesco. "I would like you to meet a friend, a fellow townsman, Father Pasquale Miozza."

Father Palermo smiled at his visitor. "Pleased to meet you."

"The pleasure is mine," responded Father Pasquale.

"What brings you here?"

"I came to see my sister, who is ill. She lives in Cleveland."

"To what do I owe this visit?"

"Francesco tells me that you are always busy, but I need some advices."

"Certainly. Come inside." The two followed him into his small office.

"So tell me what you need."

Briefly the Italian monk told him what had happened in the Irish church. After listening attentively, the priest explained, "I feel the need to update you a little on the history of the Catholic Church in America. Things are improving, but it would appear that Mother Church, God forgive me, accepts only the rich Irish, excluding us Italians, who are considered subordinate to them. It's a prejudice created partly by ignorance, which is hard to eradicate, though we Italians have also contributed to it."

"Meaning what?" asked the monk.

"Well, you know how our mothers are. When they go to church, they kiss the Madonna and caress her to ask a favor, or they talk to Saint Anthony—'Dear Saint Anthony, find a job for my son.' Their requests are more like threats, because if they don't get the right answer, they go straight to the most powerful—Jesus. For the Irish, this way of praying is pagan. You can't entirely fault them for this."

"I can see that the Irish do not understand the strength of a prayer," the monk conceded. "It is the faith that creates miracles. It was Christ himself who told his listeners, 'You believe because you see, but blessed are they who believe without seeing.'"

"But, Father Palermo," protested Francesco, "it isn't fair to judge people this way."

"Of course not," agreed the priest, "but these problems go much deeper. You have to understand that the Italian immigrants of the first half of the nineteenth century, almost up to 1880, were regarded by Rome as dissidents, revolutionaries. Even later, toward the end of the century, many of them were considered dangerous anarchists, because the Church regarded intellectuals as anticlerical. Take the examples of Joseph Ciancabilla, Henry Malatesta, Luigi Galleani, Joe Ettor, and Arturo Giovannitti. Any of them would have been considered *persona non grata* by the Catholic Church, which was controlled by the Irish clergy. But Giovannitti and his followers rejected such injustices. In 1917, because of labor union activities, they were denounced under the Espionage Act. The world of the powerful saw them as a threat. This attitude culminated in the sentencing of innocent people like Sacco and Vanzetti.

"Years ago a poet illustrated the hateful tenor of the times with these distasteful words:

They're only a couple o' damn dagos!
Now me: I am an American, I am…
Send them up, say I,
Show them that our courts is American.
We don't get our laws from Italy.
We don't care whether they done it or not.
To hell with them!
They are dagos.

"I can easily understand what you are saying, Father," said Francesco, "but what is puzzling me is the intolerance against us Italians now, in 1949."

The priest regarded him thoughtfully. "Look, it is a much bigger problem than it seems, but I will do my best to explain. First of all, you should know that, for the Irish people, the priest is the symbol of their freedom. They fled from their homeland and followed him across the ocean. On Sundays here, church attendance is 90 to 95 percent, about the same as it was in Ireland at the time of the struggles against the Protestant oppressors. When the Catholic Irish arrived in America, they were denounced as enemies of the Republic. Their churches were burned, and men who were believed to be members of a foreign conspiracy were lynched. From 1835 on, the political climate was so extremely hostile to the Catholic Irish that in 1844, in Philadelphia, members of the Native American political party attacked several Catholic churches, reducing St. Michael's and St. Augustine's to ashes. In fact, the Native American Movement Party, in 1835, wanted to deport all Irishmen from America for being papists. Later, the Know Nothing Party, which opposed all Catholics and foreigners, fought to strip all the Irish Catholics of their United States citizenship, declaring them non-citizens and proclaiming 'America for the Americans.' Therefore, for the Irish in this country, the Church represents the unity from which they derive their strength, just as it did in their dear Ireland."

"And now we are the ones discriminated against," concluded Francesco.

With an open-armed shrug, Father Palermo replied, "The oppressed become the oppressors. We Italians are more divided than the Irish, and we have been more divided since the fall of the Roman Empire fifteen hundred years ago. We are more individualistic—only twenty-five percent of us attend church with any regularity. This is why my parish is very modest in comparison to the Irish ones."

Father Pasquale and Francesco, who had been following Father Palermo's every word with obvious interest, encouraged him to go on.

The priest willingly obliged. "In defense of our fellow countrymen, I have to say that in Italy in the past, we priests were not seen as spiritual leaders, as were our Irish colleagues, but as oppressors. We were deemed to be the allies of the rich, protectors of the dons, like Don Abbondio and Don Rodrigo, even though it was understood that we were supposed to be on the side of the poor and innocent, like Renzo and Lucia—as Alessandro Manzoni, the greatest Italian novelist of the 1800s, described in *Promessi Sposi* (*The Betrothed*). It was an abominable deed to help the rich at the expense of the poor. But in Italy those in high levels have always crushed those below them."

Father Palermo was right. He told them about Booker T. Washington, a great African American educator, who had this to say about his trip to southern Italy in 1910: "The Negro is not the farthest down. The conditions of the colored farmer in the most backward parts of the southern states in America, even where he has the least education and the least encouragement, are incomparably better than the conditions and opportunities of the agricultural population in Sicily."

The truth that was coming out in the sage words of the good father was, for Francesco, another step forward. Grace had planted the seeds of his first doubts, and what Mr. Conti had said about America made them grow. He wanted to remember the name of that black educator. He was learning things that a year's schooling could not have taught him.

"We Italians still suffer from preconceived ideas," continued Father Palermo. "We cannot shake off this old myth of the Mafia, full of prejudices, disseminated by irresponsible people and especially by the media. Our history has perhaps contributed to our lack of religious conviction, which is in such direct contrast to the orthodox faith of the Irish and the Polish. But some of the hostile allegations, besides being undeserved, are ridiculous. For example, here I am known as Father Mafioso." That wisecrack brought smiles to the faces of the two listeners, who were immediately embarrassed for having reacted so.

The priest then told them about a criminal named Al Capone, who became a scapegoat, always identified only as an Italian in a criminal system that, without the direct complicity of the police and the judicial apparatus, could not operate. For years the police closed their eyes to the Irish criminality, as long as they could get information leading to the annihilation of the Italian-American Mafia.

"The media have done their best to spread all these stereotypes and prejudices," Father Palermo added.

He then began leafing through some papers and looked up when he found what he was looking for. "I want to share with you something an Irish friend wrote to me: 'My mother was Irish, from the Sligo County, and making booze was a family tradition. In Ireland everybody makes his own stuff. When prohibition hit, we had to watch out for cops, even though some of our best customers were cops. Sometimes they would not pay for their drinks, but mostly we would take care of them, you know, if they were working the beat. When we brought in barrels of beer, we would give the beat cop a dollar a barrel if he was watching. This kind of thing was going on at every level. If the prohibition agents were going to raid us, we would usually get a call from the police captain at the desk telling us ahead of time. Everyone was on the take back then, all the way up to the mayor of New York Jimmy Walker. In fact, we used to make deliveries to his house every week.'"

The two young Italians were fascinated by this information. They were being baptized into a new religion of American dirty politics.

"Unbelievable," said Francesco.

"Well," continued the good father, "the media failed in its duty to tell the world that it was America that was violent, not the Italians who were being painted as evil because of a few criminal compatriots. During the search for gold in the Far West and Alaska, many unfortunate immigrants were eliminated by unscrupulous men who wanted them out of their way, and in the South poor immigrants had to defend themselves against lynching mobs. The government itself should have intervened on behalf of these oppressed, frustrated, and defenseless people. Yet, the newspapers continued to devote their front page to the Mafia, when I personally could mention many Irish, Jewish, black, and other criminal elements whose adverse publicity would always be buried in the back pages—assassins like Abe Redes, Moe Dalitz, Dandy Phil Kastel, Lepke Buchalter, or James Moran, the Irishman who controlled a good part of Chicago."

The seemingly inexhaustible priest had much more to say: "A half-million Americans of Italian descent—four percent of the American population—suffered a mortality rate of ten percent during the Second World War. Among them were some genuine heroes, including twelve who received the highest honor, the Congressional Medal of Honor. Sergeant John Basilone was the only enlisted Marine to receive both the Congressional Medal of Honor and the Navy Cross during the war. In 1942, for three days, Sergeant Basilone, armed with a machine gun, single-handedly fought an entire Japanese regiment at Guadalcanal. General Douglas MacArthur called him 'a one-man army.' Basilone was then asked to go back home to participate in rallies and parades to raise money for war bonds. But his patriotism compelled him to return to the war, and in 1945 he was killed at the Battle of Iwo Jima."

Francesco and his visitor had come to Father Palermo for an explanation as to why they had been rebuffed by the Irish church. They had received far more than that; they had gotten a civic lesson unlike any that could be found in American textbooks.

62 After more than two years of searching, Iuccio had still not found work. He felt caught between the hammer and the anvil, Italy and America. He would have to decide soon whether to stay; otherwise, he would lose his permanent job in Italy.

Mr. Mazzarino, the Ceppones' friend, used to tell Iuccio, "This is not the fantasy land of Pinocchio or Peter Pan. Here, one either grows fast or he dies quickly."

Iuccio had hit bottom. He was humiliated and stripped of his self-respect. Useless were all the comforts that Angela provided for him. Frustrated, Iuccio continued to humiliate Assunta, as if she were not the mother of his wife and grandmother of his children. Furthermore, his abusive wisecracks directed at his mother-in-law had created a mistrustful and intolerable relationship, where everyone was holding his breath, fearing that some day Giosué, Iuccio's father-in-law, would lose his patience.

Iuccio had arrived at a crossroad, but which path could he choose? Returning to Italy without his dear ones, without his beloved family, would mean a solitary life. To stay in America would mean to die a bit at a time.

Meanwhile, at home Angela and Assunta were preparing a big party in honor of Benjamin, who was receiving the highest award at school—the Award of the Year. He had distinguished himself not only by his academic achievements, but also by his election to the National Honor Society, which admitted only exemplary students with the highest grades. For his work on *The Iron Star*, he was cited as the best editor of a school newspaper in the state of Ohio. For these honors he received scholarships that would pay his tuition at the prestigious Case Western Reserve University in Cleveland.

Because the graduation class was so large that year, the ceremony took place in the school stadium. The Ceppones, Tottis, and Salvatos sat in the tenth row, a few steps from the stage, where several dignitaries and honor students were seated. Everyone rose as soon as the national anthem began. Then the principal walked to the podium and began his address:

"Monsignor Abbey, members of the Board of Education, teachers, class of 1949, kind ladies and gentlemen, Welcome to this extraordinary event in the history of our alma mater. We have the largest number of graduating students who will take their places this September in universities throughout our land. Today, June 15, 1949, one of these young people will be recognized for having distinguished himself in a particular way by earning in just two years in the United States of America the highest honors of this class. Two years ago, he arrived from Italy, having been separated from his mother and grandparents by the tragedy of the Second World War. He determined to learn our language, the mastery of which is mirrored in his capacity as editor of *The Iron Star*, for which he was highly praised during the scholastic year. This big event is part of our tradition of many successful immigrants. Reaching the goal of graduating is a difficult undertaking. But it is not rare in a system such as ours, where there are no social or economic barriers, only the spirit of total equality. I introduce to you the student who, more than any other, represents our values of discipline, honesty, and mutual respect."

As he turned the podium over to Benjamin, the crowd rose in applause. Then Benjamin began addressing the crowd. "It is of great comfort to have my mother, my father, my brother, my grandparents, my uncles, and my cousin near in this land. This is a dream that I had nurtured for eight long years in my languishing heart, longing for that faraway affection, that most desired maternal love."

The crowd, already aware of his past, stood up again, but this time there were tears mixed in with the applause.

"Why are you are crying?" Iuccio asked Angela.

"I will tell you later," she replied. "Joy sometimes brings tears, and right now I want to enjoy the moment."

Benjamin continued, "I want first of all to thank all my teachers for their tireless help and patience, and the principal for his great wisdom. And special thanks to my friends for their brotherhood. Today each of us will take a different path, and I want to wish all of you great success in the future. But I also want you to know that my house will always be yours. At this time I would like to take the opportunity to thank my parents and my good grandparents for their guidance and their many sacrifices. And I would like the world to know that, without any doubt, my

American dream has come true. Therefore, I thank this country that I will love and hold in my memories and warmly in my heart for the opportunities and immense happiness I have been privileged to have here."

The ceremony ended with the benediction by Monsignor Abbey and the tradition of the graduates' throwing their hats into the air as if to say, "Free at last!" The celebrants now turned their thoughts to the various parties they would attend that evening. Iuccio's relatives went home, while Benjamin rode off with some of his friends in a car decorated with a banner that read, JUST GRADUATED. A little after six, the telephone rang at the Ceppones', where everyone was busy preparing for the reception that was to take place at seven o'clock. The call was from Saint Elizabeth Hospital in Youngstown, reporting that Benjamin, with three of his friends, had been involved in a car accident. Angela and Iuccio immediately took a taxi to the hospital and, from the first minute they saw their son, did not leave his side. The early diagnosis called for a recovery in perhaps one month. But neither their prayers nor those of the whole city were enough to save him. Three days later he died under the eyes of all his loved ones. He had received severe injuries to chest and limbs. The doctors protected themselves by saying that complications had set in.

The official report was that he had been found under the car seat, from which it had taken half an hour to extract him. Judging by the tracks left by the wheels, the police determined that excessive speed had caused the crash. All the local newspapers devoted the front page to this tragedy, recounting the Totti family's story of many years of suffering and separation brought on by the war.

At the funeral home the casket was flanked by two mountains of flowers and telegrams. Among the mourners, all immovable like statues, were his white, black, Asian, and Indian companions, mirroring the true face of America. Also in the crowd were public, scholastic, and religious figures, including Protestant ministers, Catholic and Greek Orthodox priests, and rabbis.

Angela began crying uncontrollably, but with dignity. All the comforting words of the priest could not give solace to her grief. Iuccio seemed destroyed, absent, transported somewhere else by an invisible power. A female classmate tried to read a message that she had written for the occasion, but got lost in her emotions. And John was there, his dearest friend and the only survivor. He had caused the tragedy by driving too fast. He walked with a noticeable limp, and now had to live with the heavy burden of the shameful *mea culpa*. He could only say, "I am destroyed."

Angela, helped by Grace, and Iuccio, by Francesco, came out of the church and entered the lead car of the long procession. The hearse first passed in front of the school, where, on a suspended white and purple banner over the main door, Benjamin's companions had expressed their feelings with these simple words: "Thanks, Benjamin. To you we owe the happiest days." But one could hear the sobbing of girls.

At the cemetery it seemed for an instant as if the world wanted to stop, as if it wanted to prevent the continuing flow of tears and terrible cries coming from Angela. Grace was doing her best to comfort her. Italo was being consoled by his grandparents, while Iuccio walked in a daze through the verdant cemetery among dozens of roses and countless other flowers that gave the impression of a lawn garden rather than a final resting place.

For Iuccio and Angela, the unexpected death of their son struck them like a violent hurricane. They were in agony. Iuccio's former tempestuous character was now replaced by a docile but nervous one. Someone observed him one day trying to light two cigarettes at the same time without realizing it. In the following weeks, the only thing that stayed with him, other than the terrible pain, was his anger over his past decisions.

Angela tried to tell her husband that his suffering was purifying him, as if Benjamin had sacrificed himself in order for them to find peace. Indeed, it seemed strange that Iuccio, who, after months of suffering and isolation, now appeared almost serene. Perhaps he had finally seen the fragility of life. He had taken refuge in God's temple where, for the first time, he found tranquillity.

He now looked the future in its eyes, concentrating on Italo, who was getting ready to attend Ohio State University in Columbus. He did not want the American Dream to become the American Nightmare for his living son. He wanted HOPE to become Italo's goal.

63 The next year Francesco graduated from Memorial High School in Campbell, Ohio, even though school had not been easy for him. After a difficult entrance examination, he was accepted at nearby Youngstown State, where he could obtain a college education at a reasonable cost.

More than two years had gone by since his arrival in America. Despite numerous difficulties, Francesco had reached his first goal—entering an institution of higher learning. Time had passed quickly, almost masking those boring days of the past when, as a child without his father, each day seemed an eternity. Now he was seeing more clearly his own American Dream. It was not his intellectual ability that distinguished him from others; rather it was his healthy and stable character, disciplined by a vigorous moral code. He regarded his inner life as more important than the external one, a philosophy that paralleled Grace's practical and simple one.

Francesco knew that, in order to climb, it was necessary to continue looking up, emulating those who had reached high levels, like Fiorello LaGuardia, the first American of Italian descent to reach national prominence when he became mayor of New York City. He was the David who took on the Goliath of criminality in one of the largest cities of the world. But he, too, had to endure bitter experiences, beginning with the contempt of his peers when he arrived in America at the age of ten. "Hey, Fiorello, you dago, where is your monkey?" they would jeer, likening him to the organ grinder who was going through their neighborhood. Was this the invisible enemy that controlled racism through images, as Father Palermo used to say?

Fiorello hated the word "dago." He had a particular dislike for the city of Omaha, Nebraska, because it had a district called "Dago Hill" where some Italian immigrants had ventured to settle in 1863, a place where the law of the Wild West was enforced and justice was rendered on the spot by self-appointed sheriffs.

Fiorello was also outspoken on the subject of local government abuse of the "Indios." "I saw hungry Indians and Indian kids watch us while we munched on a Kansas apple or ate cookies Mother baked. I knew, even as a child, that the government in Washington provided food for all those Indians, but also that the politicians sold these rations to miners and even to general stores, robbing Indians of the food the government provided for them and often calling them savages.

Francesco, by now, understood that he would have to adjust to living in his adopted country, loving her more like a good stepmother than a real mother. Episodes of discrimination and injustice remained engraved in his mind. However, his outlook on life would be reassured by reading poems like Vincent Benet's "Nightmare at Noon":

> *Oh, yes, I know the faults and the other side,*
> *The lyncher's rope, the bought justice,*
> *The wasted land,*
> *The scales on the leaf, the bores in the corn,*
> *The finks with their clubs, the gray sky of*
> *Relief,*
> *All the long shame of our hearts and the*
> *Long disunion.*
> *I am merely remarking—as a country, we try.*
> *As a country, I think we try.*

64 As might have been expected, Francesco's first year in college was very difficult. The language continued to be an obstacle despite the encouragement of teachers who recognized his good qualities and his potential as a teacher. During the first semester of the second year, his English professor, Karl Krites, after listening to his speech on fascism, privately told Francesco that one day he could become a good university professor. These encouraging words inspired him in trying to bring his second goal to fruition, finishing college.

He had also enlisted in the Reserve Officer Training Corps (R.O.T.C.), which he had undertaken more out of financial necessity than any military ambition. More than anything else, this strategy made it possible for him to acquire an education and, perhaps, to serve in the army of his adopted country.

Despite Francesco's academic progress, his relationship with Grace was cooling down. Being very busy with school, Francesco didn't give much weight to Grace's diminished affection. He thought that she was going through a little crisis, but nothing else.

He would be forced to face the truth one autumn day while he sat in her house, waiting for her to return from work— just as he had done many times before. Mrs. Ricchiuti told him gently that perhaps the relationship with her daughter should end. "We have talked in the family," she explained. "We are living in the fifties, and it does not seem practical to wait for so many years to get married. It is very difficult for us to tell you these things, because you are like a son to me. So I beg you to see our point of view."

These words penetrated his heart with the piercing force of a dagger. At that moment Grace arrived. Looking at her mother, she immediately knew what had transpired.

"Mother, leave us alone, please," she begged.

This living room, where peace and love once reigned,

had been transformed into a battleground that left him emotionally exhausted.

Grace turned to face Francesco. "Yes, it is true. We have talked in the family, but the reason why I have not told you anything is that I know you too well. I did not want to distract you from your studies at the university."

What he had heard was the holy truth, but that kind of reasoning succeeded in satisfying only his mind. His heart was another matter. No logic would mitigate what it felt. It was an insupportable solution.

"What do you propose that we do?" he asked.

"Let us give each other some space for two or three months."

"Meaning what?" Francesco found such a prospect frightening.

"Not to see each other for some time."

"But what will that help us to do?"

"To see how things go," Grace replied calmly.

Francesco saw that arguing with Grace would be counterproductive. Her mind was made up. He took his jacket, said goodbye to Mrs. Ricchiuti, and left the house without another word.

That evening during supper his mother asked him, "What's with your bad mood?"

"I am not feeling too good," was all he was willing to say.

In a few days Iuccio, Angela, and the rest of the family came to know the real reason for his unusual behavior.

Christmas Day arrived. While his parents went to Mass, Francesco, with a leaden heart, remained at home to read. Upon returning from church, his mother told him that Grace had wished her a Merry Christmas, kissing her Italian style, on both cheeks. He pretended not to be interested, but his mood betrayed him. He continued to read throughout the day, but without understanding anything. Nothing changed in the next two months. His mind kept wandering. How would this end? Was it not their destiny to be together when they loved each other so much? These questions were clarified on a misty evening in early February when Francesco ventured out into the cold to visit some friends. Suddenly he met Grace face-to-face at the corner of a building. The sight of her dazzled his senses. Neither of them was able to resist the overwhelming desire to embrace, to kiss each other for a long time. It was obvious that they would not be separated ever again.

Shortly afterward, on Valentine's Day, the traditional holiday for lovers, Francesco and Grace went out for a night of dancing at the beautiful ballroom of Idora Park in Youngstown. As the music of Guy Lombardo and his Royal Canadians filled the air, Francesco took Grace's hand and slipped a heart-shaped engagement ring onto her finger. He told her gently that this act united them forever, according to St. Valentine.

"What do you mean, 'according to St. Valentine'?" she asked.

"The story goes that St. Valentine, a Roman priest, secretly married couples after Emperor Claudio issued an edict prohibiting marriages, because, once married, men refused to go to war. For us, it means that, since this is Valentine's Day, we are now secretly married."

At that point she kissed him, a kiss that sealed their union as much as a marriage certificate. And then she said: "I love the ring, but its true value is its symbol."

Mrs. Ricchiuti was happy about their reconciliation, but also a bit guilty about having caused such grief, however temporary, to the young man whom she liked so very much. Unfortunately, she did not have much time to enjoy this happy reunion, for she died of cancer some months later.

65 Life for Iuccio was going from bad to worse. When he went out looking for a job, he felt as though he were begging for alms. Yet he kept remembering Mr. Mazzarino's words, that only fools couldn't make it

in America. One day he took those words to heart and decided to move his entire family to Philadelphia in hopes of starting a new life, one that would have its sacrifices but would also bring him self-respect. In the City of Brotherly Love, Iuccio had an important cousin, Nick Marconi, who was vice-president of a clothing factory.

Nick immediately put him to work in the factory. After much trial and error that resulted in the loss of thousands of dollars, Iuccio gradually learned the art of cutting cloth for suits. Finally the idealistic caterpillar metamorphosed into a pragmatic butterfly. His hard expression and sharp features softened; his manner grew more refined. He was no longer the man who wanted to have his cake and eat it too. He was ready to live his daily life as an honest, responsible, hard-working man. Now he hated the deadheads who only made noise, as he once had done. Now thinner, he became more self-confident. And one of his positive traits resurfaced: the ability to laugh and make others laugh. His wisecracks, still clever but no longer cruel, made him very popular with his co-workers.

66 Francesco graduated from Youngstown State on June 1, 1954, with a degree in Spanish, Latin and French. Having also been commissioned a second lieutenant in the United States Army, he knew the day was near when he would be called to service and he wondered to what part of the world he would be sent. Now that the Korean conflict was over, he would have to serve only one year. This was a comfort to him, but not to the families, who simply found it distressing that Francesco should receive his orders so soon after the planned June wedding.

Everything for the wedding had been arranged to the last detail when Francesco received a telegram from Italy announcing the death of his brother-in-law, Saverio, his first guide in life whom he had learned to love and respect. It was not the first time that hc had suffered a loss. He had struggled even more with the deaths of poor Benjamin and Grace's mother.

However, on June 12, the wedding went on as planned. The bridegroom, wearing a simple gray suit and a brilliant white shirt in striking contrast to his wavy black hair, waited with much dignity for his bride in the new Saint Lucy's Church, which he and other Italians had helped to build. The bridesmaids wore dresses that were simple, yet elegant, reflecting the simplicity of the bride and the ceremony itself. Among those present were his best man, cousin Italo Totti, who, along with his wife, Pat, had arrived from Maine to join other family members for the celebration.

Finally Grace appeared, in a white dress, the symbol of her twenty-four years of pure existence. Showing a bit of a Mona Lisa smile, she readied herself for being photographed from every corner of the church. Father Palermo officiated in a brief but solemn ceremony before the large crowd that had gathered to honor the joyful conclusion to this sentimental story, which had been unfolding for seven years.

After the benediction, Grace placed some flowers at the feet of the Virgin Mary and then let her husband guide her to the front of the church where the photographer recorded their most important moments. Afterwards, they were led to the garden of the church, where a long table of appetizers had been prepared for the guests. There were several bottles of Louis Rederer champagne ready for a toast. Telegrams arrived, wishing them well. Among them was one from Iuccio, which had been written in English by Angela. Iuccio's absence surprised everyone, but his newly acquired work ethic made him unwilling to be absent from his job on a Saturday.

When the celebration was over, Francesco and Grace left on their honeymoon. They had planned to drive to Florida. One day during the trip she happened to look at their marriage certificate, and was delighted to see that it read "Mr. and Mrs. Frank and Grace Salvato." It made her feel good to be called Mrs. Grace Salvato. Her new husband would need time to adjust to being called Frank. He had changed his name, because nobody was able to pronounce his former name well.

They spent the first night in Atlantic City, where Miss America is crowned each year, and after a day in the sun Grace was burned so badly that she was unable to walk. Unfortunately, no medical attention made her well enough to enjoy the rest of her honeymoon, and they were forced to return home. Frank lifted her gingerly from the car, and while he was carrying her, looking like a lobster, into the house, she started to scream. Their Greek neighbor, Macrilla, rushed out, and not knowing what had happened, folded her hands in prayer and started to question Frank. "Franky, Franky, what have you done to my butterfly, Gracie?" She had every reason to ask such a question. After all Macrilla had watched her grow into a lovely, delicate creature. And now "Bad Franky" had brought her home roasted and half-crippled.

67 Grace paid dearly for her sunbathing in Atlantic City. Two weeks passed and still she could hardly move. Her mother-in-law, Maria, helped her continually, and even Macrilla lent a hand sometimes. In a few days Frank would have to leave for military duty. The tree of life that the two hearts had planted a few days before, on June 12, had immediately taken deep roots, and to disturb it now was unfortunate timing. Frank's departure would have provoked a much more severe crisis had it not been that his military career was going to be of short duration—a year of separation, with the possibility of his coming home at Christmas for ten days.

On the morning of June 30, Frank left for the base at Fort Bliss, Texas, in the company of three other soldiers with whom he would spend the next few months in training. Saying goodbye to Grace had been a difficult but tender moment for Frank, who left her with a kiss and an "I love you."

It was nine o'clock in the evening when the four soldiers

arrived in the city of St. Louis, Missouri, so they immediately went to a hotel. The clerk informed them that he could accommodate the three whites in their party, but that Johnson, the black officer, would have to find another hotel. The soldiers were shocked, but they immediately understood the implications and left in protest. Three of them flashed an erect middle finger from a closed right fist. Frank showed the clerk the whole right arm, a much more provocative Italian gesture that the employee probably did not understand.

The military-camp experience of the year before had trained them for open-space living, so they encamped in a nearby park. For Frank, the experience in St. Louis was a bitter reminder of the cruelty of another time, when Benito Mussolini was in power.

In the morning they went on their way, traveling for many miles on straight Texan highways without seeing a living soul. At one point, a sandstorm occurred, nearly burying them within a few minutes. With much apprehension they decided they had better stop. When the weather cleared, later than they had imagined, they continued to El Paso, the city nearest to Fort Bliss.

After five months of military theory, Frank had a few days of leave and went home to spend Thanksgiving, rather than Christmas, with the family. Upon returning to the base, he spent seven more months shuttling between his base of Fort Bliss and nearby White Sand, New Mexico, where his company went early every morning for maneuvers and experiments.

During all these months the newlyweds corresponded so frequently that the mail carrier at the base could put Frank's letters from Grace in the correct box with hardly a glance at the box number on the envelope. Their telephone calls intensified after Grace announced in December that their first "twig" would be born in August. The desire to be with her and anxiety about her welfare made him sweat much more than did the 120 degrees of desert heat. In seven years, they had never been separated for such a long period of time.

Frank was surprised by the affectionate and modest behavior of his fellow officers He had assumed that their training at the Citadel, the "West Point of the South," in South Carolina, might make them condescending toward the ROTC graduates. But, in fact, these officers were always joking good-naturedly about his accent, and he, in turn, teased them about their strange drawl. They were different from the supervisors or bosses of civilian life, some of whom suffered from a superiority complex.

He was also surprised that the government had such trust in him, knowing that he had been active in the Fascist Party until its fall. And yet he went on to receive his commission as second lieutenant, proof that America had faith in his professed allegiance to the Stars and Stripes.

The pristine environment of western Texas reminded him of his native land—hot and dry during the day, but cool and clear at night so that one could see the firmament in its full glory, the huge diamonds fixed in the sky and the brilliant sapphires falling to earth. His military career was almost a vacation for him. When he returned home, he was welcomed as a hero, with all the fanfare awarded a veteran who had known battle.

68 Frank's experience as a part-time laborer during his first seven years in America made him keenly aware of the choices he faced upon graduation. But there was no doubt in his mind about what he wanted to do. He would not grow old in the mill world where war veterans were favored with lucrative jobs in the steel industries. Now that he had fulfilled his military obligation, he would reap the fruit of his sacrifices and become a teacher.

His university counselor advised him to submit an application to the Youngstown School District, where there would most likely be openings in September. A few weeks later Frank received a request for him to appear for an interview on July 5 in the office of the superintendent of Mahoning County.

The interview was not a cordial one. It lasted no more than half an hour. At the end, the superintendent told him, "Your curriculum vitae is impressive, but I have to tell you that all the teachers in our city are American-born. For the moment we are not accepting foreigners."

Frank was stunned by this affront. It was difficult for him to rein in his emotions. Such a discriminatory act could not have been any clearer. The message was as heavy and offensive as the rude language in which it was delivered. The true character of the superintendent showed on his face, which, for Frank, would forever symbolize the perpetuation of bigotry.

With a tight mouth and a heart aching for revenge, for a victory of his own, Frank left Dr. Smith's office. As a parting gesture of admonition, Frank managed only to arch his eyebrows. His curse was visible, written all over his face, and not even his profuse sweating could erase it. He knew that sometimes in life the strong violate the weak. Had he been another scapegoat? Was not this episode another form of "lynching"? He felt a kinship with the Italians who were lynched in Tallulah, Louisiana, in 1889, in New Orleans in 1891, and in Walsenburg, Colorado, in 1895.

Almost in tears, he thought again about the Founding Fathers and their fear of the misuse of power, and about Patrick Henry who had said: "Give me liberty or give me death." How sad! These men had put their heads on the line, risking their lives to ensure justice. Were all their sacrifices in vain? The scales of justice seemed to have been tipped once again in favor of the strong.

How did one deal with such irrational mentality, he wondered. How could a person get away with being so uncouth, so arrogant and bigoted? How could anyone dismiss him as a foreigner when he had served in the United States Army? Was there anyone who could help him, anyone he could talk to? His wife was at work. Everybody was at work. His sisters, his relatives, his oldest friends—all of them were in Italy. For an instant at least, Italy seemed better, more just.

But even that was an illusion.

Such thoughts plagued him for days. Being married now, he felt even more the heavy burden of his responsibility. Even though Frank did not know how to cope with such a stressful episode, he knew he had to remain calm. His only remedy in the past, when he wanted to rid himself of the emotional tensions of the day, had been some form of exercise, especially jogging. So he began a regimen of running, dissipating all the poison in his hurting mind. Until then, the struggle against injustice had been something he read about in books; now, discrimination had directly manifested itself in the form of the superintendent who had called him "foreigner" as if that meant something criminal. Frank's bitterness gave way to pride and he was inspired to take on his real mission: to fight bigotry at all costs.

The Second World War in Italy now seemed to have been a true apprenticeship for the future battles of life. He could see that discrimination was his enemy, the true obstacle on the way to success. He was ready to fight it, encouraged by his university teacher, Dr. William Cox, who advised him, "When the doors are not opened wide enough, it is time to double the efforts."

He began sending out many applications, making inquiries everywhere, knocking on door after door. He got his first teaching assignment at Brookfield High, not too far from home. In the meantime, to ensure future success, he also enrolled at the famous language school of Middlebury College, in Vermont, to pursue a master's degree in Spanish during the summer.

69 After a visit to the doctor, Frank and Grace got news that made them very happy. Grace wasted no time in getting ready for the arrival of the little prince or princess.

On August 12, 1955, she gave birth to an extraordinarily beautiful child. It was a splendid day. Now, after getting married and finding a job, Frank had achieved his third objective—to start a family.

Two weeks later the child was baptized "Frank, Jr." Sister-in-law Lucy was named godmother and Italo, godfather. The rest of the Tottis participated in the celebration: Iuccio and Angela, from Philadelphia, and Italo's wife, Pat, from Maine. People kept coming and going that day to admire Frankie's beauty. This was a rare get-together for the Totti and the Salvato families; because they lived in different cities, they communicated only on special holidays.

Iuccio's temples had silvered, perhaps from his troubled past, but he seemed at peace with himself. His charm had returned, as had his desire to live. One could see that he was madly in love with Angela. This crazy juvenile love had first reappeared in the aftermath of Benjamin's devastating tragedy and was re-enforced by living in the City of Brotherly Love. Iuccio had become a master of piecework in tailoring and was pleased to have a well-paying job. He even enjoyed working on Saturdays, when he was paid double. He told Frank: "If it had not been for Benjamin's misfortune, I would feel really happy in this country. Now I have only you and Italo, so I want the two of you to love each other." And, in fact, Italo and Frank felt more like true brothers than cousins. The two were so similar that Italo chose to enter the same profession as Frank, which not only had an ethical value for them both, but also gave them a certain normality and steadiness in life that was important for their family's healthy growth.

70

One day, some months later, a worried Maria asked Grace to take her little angel to the physician.

"Mama, we took him only a month ago," she responded a bit defensively. But then, knowing her mother-in-law to open her mouth only when necessary, she asked, "Why that question, Mother?"

"I hope I am wrong, but I do not see certain movements in Frankie," the older woman answered.

"Mother, he is only two months old. What do you want him to do?" she protested angrily. Grace had submitted to all the prescribed clinical tests during her pregnancy and had taken all the precautions suggested by the physician. She had even given up her only vice—drinking coffee.

Nevertheless, Grace began to have doubts. That day, upon returning from school, Frank found his wife upset.

"Don't you see what a beautiful little angel we have? He cannot be more normal," Frank said soothingly. But his reassurance was in vain. She calmed down only after he promised to make an appointment with the specialist Dr. Siegel.

They did not sleep the whole night, thinking about the observations of Frank's wise mother. At one o'clock in the afternoon of the following day, with Frankie in Grace's arms, they entered the physician's private office. After a few minutes the confirmation came. "During birth Frankie suffered a lack of oxygen for a few seconds, damaging his brain," the physician told them in simple terms. Grace's arms and legs began trembling. The doctor immediately gave her a sedative, but there was no medicine that could assuage that heavy, painful *Via Dolorosa*. Frank embraced her, comforting her, pressing his chest against hers as if he wanted to melt their two bodies into one. The love between them would strengthen, just as it had united Iuccio and Angela after the tragic loss of Benjamin.

Returning home by car, the two heartbroken parents gave vent to their emotions. Grace kept weeping, and Frank wondered aloud, "How is it possible that such a just God would cause such undeserved misery? How can He be so cruel? How can He remain so impassive toward two pure hearts? Can there truly be a God, the Highest?"

As Frank drove on, Grace sat close beside him, kissing her little angel over and over again, as if to reassure him that the physician's advice to put him away was out of the question. "You are mine and I will never abandon you," she whispered to him softly. She kept him in her arms like a jewel in a velvet box, bathing and washing him with her tears and then wiping him with her caressing face.

In the following days and weeks, Frank and Grace, hoping for the best, took their baby son to a famous clinic in Cleveland, then to Pittsburgh, and finally to Boston. Every nurse fell in love with the child, but hope for his improvement was decreasing.

Every day Frank would return from school and ask the same question, "Any news?" Grace's tear-stained face would be his answer. The young parents were absorbed in a drama that engulfed them in silence. Nevertheless, misfortune brought them closer together than ever before, strengthening their love and their mutual trust, with Frankie as the center of their world. At those times when Frank gave in to his despair, cursing their fate in bitter language, Grace would become sad.

"How can you doubt the existence of Our Creator?" she asked him one day, trying to reason with him. "He creates, He takes away, and He disposes according to His design, which we can't understand."

Frank was sitting down with his head between his hands, lost in thought, as she came over to caress and then embrace him. She was right. Although she was a worrier, she was the stronger of the two. She was able to face problems, however painful, and she had the inner resources to resolve them.

Good news finally came from one of their doctors, Dr. Danciff, informing them that Frankie's problem was not genetic and encouraging them to have other children.

71 In 1958 Frank transferred from Brookfield High to the Youngstown School District, where Latin teachers were in great demand and the pay was better. He was returning to the battleground where Dr. Smith had appeared to win the first battle. Frank's return was a resounding

defeat for Dr. Smith, but Frank never went to the man's office to claim his victory.

Frank continued his mission, striving for recognition of the culture and contributions of Italy, but the work was tortuous. Prejudices were common, and Frank was shocked to find that some of them were being re-enforced by prominent Italian intellectuals arriving in America as exiles. One of these was Giuseppe Prezzolini, a great Italian writer and former head of the Casa Italiana at Columbia University, who had this to say about the Italians in America in 1931:

> They are not Italian, because they have never been Italians. Here they have picked up some American habits, but fundamentally they have remained the same southern farmers, without culture, without language, for which, in short, the moment of their being Italian has never arrived. They left Italy before being Italians. They have been here and they have not become full Americans.

72 As foreseen by Dr. Danciff, Grace gave birth to a beautiful baby girl, Linda Maria, on January 17, 1960. The first name was to confirm her beauty, and the middle name was to honor her grandmother.

Early on, she showed herself to be very lively. One month after her birth, while in church for her baptism, she surprised everyone by holding up her head like a peacock. After seven months she began walking and saying, "Mama," reassuring the whole family and especially those two hearts that had been harboring so much worry.

Frank continued to devote much of his time to Frankie, but he also paid attention to his new daughter, often speaking to her in several languages as if he wanted to try out her intelligence. By the age of one year, Linda had learned to kiss

Frankie when Frank sang in Italian to her. She would kiss her mother when her father sang "Frère Jacques," and when he followed that with "*Frai Felipe, duermes tu, duermes tu,*" she kissed her father.

Grandfather Ricchiuti and Frank's parents came over every evening to enjoy these little shows. Their little granddaughter gave them much joy.

73 Summer vacation was approaching. Linda, now eighteen months old, was always in the park near their house, exhausting her three grandparents, who tried to play with her as she ran round and round like a little butterfly.

Grandma Maria was a bit worried about her son, even though Frank, like so many immigrants, had a strong constitution and lived by the old Roman axiom *Mens sana in corpore sano* (a sound mind, in a sound body). Although he appeared to handle his professional and family obligations without difficulty, his duodenal ulcers continued to flare up, evidence of the stress brought on by unspoken concerns about his job and his son. For days the discomfort never let up and he was losing weight. During that stressful period he ignored the medical recommendations for a stomach operation. He said to himself, "As it came, it must go," remembering the old fatalism of his forefathers when they had to face a disease.

Nevertheless, Maria suggested that he go on vacation in Italy with his wife and daughter, leaving Frankie with her. Her proposal was well received by the rest of the family. Grandmother Maria was the only one trained to put a handkerchief in Frankie's mouth to prevent him from breaking his teeth when he had convulsions, and she also knew how to administer the blessed, expensive medicine that would reduce their occurrence.

So, after fourteen years of absence, Frank returned to his

native land. When he arrived with his wife and daughter at the railroad station not far from the village of Toro, some of his old friends—including Attilio and Mercurio—were there to greet the family. Frank's appearance surprised them—he looked thin and pale. At times he had difficulty expressing himself in Italian, which he had rarely spoken during all those intervening years. Grace, on the other hand, with her rosy cheeks, seemed healthy, happy to be there, and quite willing to meet everybody. Her gentle manners reflected her modesty, and she was immediately accepted. But all eyes were centered on the little girl with them, a child frightened by so many new faces, each one wanting a kiss.

The two Americans, as Frank and Grace were called, received many warm invitations from friends, who embraced them with brotherly affection everywhere they went. One evening they were invited to a friend's house to watch a national television show featuring Toto', Italy's funniest comic. But all eyes were fixed not on Toto' but on Grace, because she was the first woman they had ever seen wearing slacks. As soon as they returned home, she was angry with Frank because he had not discouraged her from wearing what the local people considered to be provocative attire.

It was an unforgettable summer, however, for it made them feel as if they were in their own home. The simple life brought the color back to his cheeks and replenished his soul with such tranquillity that his stomach pains disappeared. After fourteen years, Frank was retracing the streets of his memory, where imagination and fantasy were often confused with reality, where fiction and history were continually intermingled. He liked the life here. Right then he knew that he would have to come back.

Coming home from their vacation, they landed in Philadelphia, where, waiting for them, were Iuccio, Angela, and their well-off relative, Nick Marconi. The visit had the atmosphere of a special event, because they had not seen one another for some time. Supper was sumptuous and the reception warm. The house had the air of a typical Italian villa with all the comforts and a garden with many roses blooming at summer's end.

During supper, Angela asked about Frankie. "Look," said Grace, "it is a cross that we carry twenty-four hours a day, but it is a beautiful one. Every day we learn something from him. He has opened our minds to a lifestyle that is very different from the way other young couples live today. He has helped us to mature, and he has made us wiser than we could have ever imagined. He is the angel that guides us daily."

"What Grace has said so clearly is the holy truth," Frank added, "and I could not have said it any better. Certainly, I would never have thought it possible to have such happiness or such peace, but I am sure that was inspired by our son. Grace never complains and endures her pains with dignity. I am the one who protested to God in blasphemy."

"Frank," cautioned his wife, hoping to avoid reviving memories of his days of rebellion against heaven.

"But things could get more complicated as the baby gains weight," interjected Mr. Marconi, who was a realist.

"We will cross that bridge when we come to it," Grace answered, a little annoyed.

"Listen," interrupted Iuccio, "why don't you move here? You know that cities provide more opportunities for the future, as Compare Dr. Santillo suggested many times to me when I was looking for a job."

"One never knows where our destiny will take us," Frank answered. However, he had taken Iuccio's suggestion to heart. It was clear that Iuccio wanted to help him—his affection for Frank and Grace was obvious. Perhaps it was a good idea to consider a transfer.

One could sense peace in Iuccio's soul as if he had established a good relationship with his Creator. Frank took pleasure in the Tottis' economic success. Like so many other immigrants, they were enjoying the fruit of their great struggles.

JANUS

74 After their reunion in Philadelphia, Frank and Iuccio reconnected with the old enthusiasm. The cloud of Benjamin's tragedy that had separated them had almost lifted, and they would often write to each other or call on the phone. After discussing Iuccio's suggestion further with Grace and then consulting some experts, Frank determined to take a one-year leave of absence from the Youngstown School District to teach at a private school in the Philadelphia area near the Tottis. Dr. Smith, his old nemesis, unwillingly granted him his transfer.

At the new school, where Frank would teach Latin and Spanish, the headmaster, Dr. Leslie Severinghouse, was the antithesis of Dr. Smith. He gave Frank's family a helping hand as soon as they arrived.

The Tottis opened their house to the Salvatos for the first few weeks. Grace had never hindered her husband's plans and followed him with unwavering faith. A month later, the Salvatos were invited to the home of Dr. Severinghouse. Such hospitality was totally different from Frank's Youngstown experience. While there, they had the pleasure of meeting Mrs. Severinghouse and her sister, Clare Booth Luce, the ambassador to Italy, whom the Italian writer Indro Montanelli had called "the Saint of Democracy."

The new environment was warm and cultured, so different from Ohio. The air was cleaner than it had been in the Ohio steel-mill valley, where smoke billowing from hundreds of chimneys made the sun a rare sight in winter or summer. They decided to take the next step: they would buy a modest house near the Tottis', large enough to accommodate Frank's parents and Grace's father.

Everybody liked the change, especially Iuccio and Angela. During the first two months the two families often enjoyed meals together. On Friday evenings they would watch the television show of Jimmy Durante, a great American comedian who always ended his program with "Goodbye, Mrs. Calabash, wherever you are."

"But who is this lady Calabash?" Grandfather Ricchiuti wanted to know.

He learned that she was a Neapolitan lady who had some boarders in her home, among whom was an aspiring comedian named Jimmy Durante. When she called these men down from the third floor to the kitchen to eat, she would always say, "Calabascia!" The comedian, who had never forgotten her kindness, immortalized her in his program as Mrs. Calabash, which in Italian dialect means "come down." Her true name was never revealed.

Iuccio and Angela had reached an enviable economic level. Every year they returned to Italy, reliving moments of their youth. After some years, however, Iuccio's right hand, which had cut so much cloth, was no longer able to do the job. The tendons were damaged, and cortisone shots could no longer lessen the swelling. He had overcome many crises in his life, but this time he seemed to be facing the end of his working career.

Soon after Iuccio stopped working, he and Angela decided to leave America to return to Italy and to enjoy the fruit of their sacrifices in a beautiful home they had purchased in Chiavari, near Genova.

75

For Grace and Frank, December 1962 was a true Calvary. Their son Frankie was hospitalized with double pneumonia. All through the Christmas season the Salvatos limited themselves to going to church and looking after that small baby, whom they had brought home from the hospital to spend Christmas with them.

The morning of New Year's Eve, Grandmother Maria went upstairs to check on Frankie, as she had often done. But this time she hurried to her daughter-in-law to report that she didn't like the way Frankie looked. "She knows Frankie well," thought Grace. "Perhaps something is different." She immediately called the doctor, who paid a brief visit and declared Frankie to be no better and no worse than the day before.

Frank accompanied the doctor to the door, but the physician lingered, asking to be paid. Frank handed the impatient doctor a twenty-dollar bill. Toward noon of that glacial day, Maria looked at the child and shook her head. "The baby doesn't look good at all."

Grace and Frank decided to take their son to the hospital rather than place another call to the doctor. After Frank spent a few minutes warming up the car, Grace settled down in the front seat with the small one on her lap and immediately embraced him to keep him warm. Frank's heart became heavy and troubled. Five minutes later, as they neared the entrance to the hospital, Grace began sobbing.

Frank stopped the car. Embracing his wife and child, he bathed them with his own tears, kissing and embracing again their firstborn, who had died in the arms of his mother without any warning. He died in peace as he had been born, without the usual cry, and his passing brought the world to a halt. While Grace kissed Frankie over and over again, Frank kept on kissing them both. In his short life, Frankie, their little angel, had radiated so much warmth in their hearts.

76 The school year finally ended. Frank's mother seemed to grieve over the loss of her little grandson, as if it signified that she was no longer needed there. She decided to return to Italy with her husband. Partly filling the void left by Frankie's death was the birth of another beautiful child, whom they called Richard.

Frank asked for another year's extension to his leave, to which the ever-hostile Dr. Smith reluctantly agreed. But Dr. Smith's letter of response was ambiguous; reading between the lines, Frank could sense a threat. Although in Italy the study of Latin was decreasing, in America it was gaining popularity as a means of raising the level of humanistic culture in an educational system dominated by a technological one. America didn't want machines to replace man completely. A nation without a soul could not be the world's leader. The spiritual components of the ancient cultures of Greece and Rome were needed. For this reason, Dr. Smith undoubtedly felt justified in threatening legal action against Frank if he did not return after this extended leave. The irony of Dr. Smith's ultimatum did not escape Frank, for this was the same man who had once, without a second thought, shown him the door. But Frank had no reason to worry now: he had already gotten another teaching assignment at Haverford High School, a well-known public school in Pennsylvania outside of Philadelphia, where he would finally find his niche in society.

At this new school, Frank noticed that about twenty-five percent of the students in his Latin and Spanish classes had Italian last names. The more he thought about this statistic, the more he dreamed that some day he might be able to teach a course in Italian. There was clearly a need within the school community. Students would come to him, wanting to have a letter translated for a relative in Italy. Or a student of music would need to have an Italian song translated. Or a teacher in the English Department would need help with an Italian poem. There were many reasons to try to convince the principal to offer a course in Italian.

He also offered the principal the idea that even American history classes could benefit. After all, Dante's language was much admired by the Founding Fathers. Thomas Jefferson, for example, was responsible for the arrival of the Italian statesman Philip Mazzei, who in turn inspired him to include in the Declaration of Independence the famous phrase "all men are created equal." (President John F. Kennedy included this footnote to history in his book *A Nation of Immigrants*.) Mazzei, a physician, agronomist and political philosopher, soon became Jefferson's great friend. In England, he had established an importing firm for Italian wines. There he met Benjamin Franklin, who suggested he come to Virginia to conduct some agricultural experiments. He accepted, arriving there with some Italian peasants. In Jefferson's library at Monticello can be found many Italian and Latin books, among which is the famous *Dei Delitti E Delle Pene* (*Crimes and Punishments*) of Cesare Beccaria, who influenced many legal minds in America.

Another selling point was that Haverford Township had a large Italian-American population. Over the span of several decades, Italian immigrants had integrated into American society with considerable economic success, an achievement that defied the expectations of numerous nay-sayers within the community. This was a new age. Immigrants no longer had to live, ten or twelve to a room, in company-owned shacks because the bosses held most of their pay—pay that was earned in the poisonous smoke of the steel mills or the black dust of the coal mines.

77 Frank knew that Italians were not alone in experiencing discrimination. Hatred toward immigrants was an old story, one that often grouped together the poor Irish, Slavs, Poles, Greeks, Russians, Scandinavians, and Germans—all of whom were fighting each other for a crumb of bread from the American loaf.

Senator John K. Shields of Tennessee once said, "The Irish will ruin this country, because they are ignorant." Meanwhile, perhaps more than any other ethnic group, Irish immigrants had given birth to many illustrious children—like John F. Kennedy, the first Catholic to break the barriers to the highest office in the land. True, other ethnic groups had been elected to high positions in their own communities, and Frank knew that some Italians had reached key positions in government.

Yet, despite the progress toward an equitable society, the wall of ostracism had not yet been demolished. For Frank it took on a more personal aspect. Too common were offensive words like dago that hurt more than swords because they penetrated the depth of one's soul. But other disparaging terms disappeared, one example being "spaghetti eaters." It had become fashionable to eat pasta, which was rapidly acquiring the status of a national dish.

Even if reality did not always reflect the hospitable message of the Statue of the Liberty to "give me your tired, your poor, your huddled masses, yearning to breathe free," even if xenophobia was still as prickly as the polar winds, immigrants had reason to hope. The American spirit, both pragmatic and idealistic, created a climate that gave rise to opportunities for a better life.

In a democratic society one cannot be indifferent. Italian-Americans viewed their culture in a spirit of renaissance and formed organizations committed to defending the rights of their fellow citizens, as well as eliminating criminal stereotypes and job discrimination. And Frank got involved in the local chapters.

These Italian-American organizations realized that votes were the best means of influencing the various powers of government. Therefore, Frank recognized the need to exhort the people in the community to participate in the elections. He also hoped that they would help him in convincing the school administration to begin courses of Italian.

Frank's pride was so strong that it energized him to go from house to house in the Italian community and present his proposal to the families. Additionally, he participated in conferences and spoke to an important organization called the Sons of Italy, to which he belonged for some time.

After seven years of continuous struggle with the school administration, he finally succeeded in his goal. He began, in 1969, to teach the first courses of Italian. They became so popular that the administration asked him to be a full-time Italian teacher.

While other governments were operating industriously for the diffusion of their culture, the Italian government showed signs of old age, dozing off on the job. Spain, France, and Germany all had funds available for teacher training so that educators could stay abreast of the latest methodologies, program new curricula, and reward their best students with prizes.

Italy, on the other hand, appeared to have one lone teacher out in the field defending the tricolor culture. Frank knew that he could count only on his own strength and that he would have to double his efforts to acquire instructional material and books. As was often the case with teachers of Italian, love of their native language and culture remained their greatest incentive to improve the image of their country in America. They could not rest on the laurels of early successes.

Italian was now making some progress among the fifty languages taught in the American schools, despite the problems of prejudice. Progress at times came at a big price. The American writer Frances Vinciguerra, for instance, acquired a certain respect from the intellectual community only after changing her name to Frances Winwar.

Frank was going forward, trying to transmit to his students the culture and values handed down by his forefathers, and illustrating and highlighting the Italian contribution to American progress. He revealed episodes that are too often ignored or falsified by American historians, as his teachers had taught him years ago after Grace had opened his eyes to the problems of discrimination.

One day he lectured on the hero of the Old and New Worlds, Giuseppe Garibaldi, who, in 1850, was in the New York home of Antonio Meucci, the inventor of the telephone later patented by Alexander Graham Bell. Frank explained to his students that Garibaldi became an American citizen and was invited by the president of the United States to participate in the Civil War, which would decide the future for the blacks. President Abraham Lincoln instructed his Secretary of State, William H. Seward, to offer Garibaldi a command as a major general in the Union Army: "I wish to proceed at once and enter into communication with the distinguished Soldier of Freedom. Tell him that this government believes his services in the present contest for unity and liberty of the American People would be exceedingly useful and that therefore he is earnestly desired and invited…. Tell him that we have abundant resources, unlimited numbers at our command, and a nation resolved to remain united and free. General Garibaldi will recognize in me, not merely an organ of the government, but an old and sincere personal friend." However, the command never came to fruition, because Garibaldi committed himself instead to the struggle in Italy where he became an instant hero for liberating his country from foreign powers and the Pope.

The students were particularly attentive when Frank told them that, on July 4, 1861, the 830-man 39th Regiment "Giuseppe Garibaldi," known as the Garibaldi Guards, marched in Washington, D.C., in a parade in front of President Lincoln, General Winfield Scott, and many other dignitaries. Among the marchers were officers of Italian descent who had participated in the Civil War. These Garibaldi Guards, made up not only of Italians but of immigrants of many nationalities, went on to distinguish themselves in the bloodiest battles of the war, from Bull Run to Appomattox.

This new vision of history that Frank was presenting created some difficulties with colleagues. In fact, that same afternoon of his lecture, another history teacher came into Frank's office. Very indignantly, she told him to stop telling students lies about American history. Frank answered her by simply saying that he could not continue to live in a world of lies. How could history mean anything if one could not get to the truth? For him, knowing the truth was the key to wisdom.

"Do you have any proof of what you are telling your students?" the history teacher demanded.

"Well, if you really care to know," Frank answered evenly, "I have a newspaper clipping of *The Illustrated London News* that you might want to read. Would you like me to make you a copy?" The teacher, by now irate and flustered, slammed the door as she left.

That same year, 1970, Frank took a trip to Italy with his students of Italian. One evening in Florence, while Frank was busy directing his students out of a restaurant toward the bus, several of them spotted a member of their group, Louis Bianco, being carried away by the police. Apparently he had made an obscene gesture with his middle finger. They immediately alerted Frank, who hurried after the officers to ask for an explanation.

"Who are you?" inquired one of the two military carabinieri.

"I am the teacher in charge."

"Documents?"

"Of course. Here is my passport." Louis, who was notably immature, would normally have forgotten his head if it weren't attached to his body, but fortunately he, too, had a passport. The policeman released the student and warned Frank, "That provocative gesture by your student could have cost him his life. You must explain to your pupils that we, the police, will shoot at anything that provokes us." The threatening tone of the carabiniere was reminiscent of the dangerous years of Italian terrorism, particularly when the Red Brigades were active. *Il Periodo del Piombo* (the Lead Period) was a time when the police shot first and asked questions later.

78 On December 27 of that same year, on a polar winter day, two old friends, Attilio Fazio and Mercurio Serpone, arrived unexpectedly from Italy and called from the Philadelphia airport. The Boston airport, their destination, was closed because of a heavy snowfall.

Grace always kept her house immaculate and charming. In the living room was a Christmas tree around which lay a nativity scene. After that phone call, she hurried to make the house even more festive for these two unexpected guests. She hung tricolor balloons on the porch, spelling out "Welcome To Our House." The next day Toni Pifalo, another childhood friend, arrived from Venezuela on a planned visit.

After a couple of days of fun and relaxation, Frank took his three friends by car to the Big Apple, New York City, where they saw a show at the famous theater La Ronde. After visiting some shops in Manhattan, they stopped at Mama Leone's, famous for its Italian cuisine. Frank ordered a table next to the window so that his friends could enjoy the view of the city. Looking at the very expensive menu, they joked about who was able to pay for it, and laughingly they all declared bankruptcy. In the meantime a waiter served them some antipasto with California wine, which everyone found to be quite good. Toni, after a second glance at the menu commented, "I wonder if we have enough money to pay for this lunch."

"I don't care," Attilio shrugged, "I will declare myself bankrupt, because I know the law of this country and it allows anyone to fail and come out clean of a messy situation."

"If that's the case," retorted Mercurio, "then I, who was born a total failure, should come out even better."

They all enjoyed the meal. At the end, while the spirited discussion on bankruptcy continued, Frank slipped away to the cashier and quietly paid the bill without his friends' knowledge of his gesture or of the final tab for the meal. After a digestive drink—compliments of the house—and an espresso, they waited for the big bill that had been a subject of so much laughter. And, of course, it never came. Even in the car while returning home, they continued to talk about their expensive lunch—obviously pleased that they did not have to pay for it—but nothing could be compared to the sumptuous supper that Grace had prepared for them that evening.

The next day, the two cousins, Toni and Mercurio, took a train for Boston, where some relatives were waiting for them. And Frank accompanied Attilio to Johns Hopkins Hospital in Baltimore to consult with the famous surgeon Dr. Albert Edgeton.

Attilio was not able to practice his profession as a physician as the result of an accident while returning home from a hunting trip. His dog, Fido, released the trigger on the doctor's rifle lying in the back seat of his car, and a bullet shot him in the right arm. Several operations in Italy had not succeeded in giving him back the use of his hand. Cold weather caused him great pain because of the poor circulation of blood.

"The doctor is on vacation," explained the secretary in good Italian upon hearing the two speaking her language. "But if you want, I can ask Dr. Jones, his assistant." Half an hour later they were shown into his office. Dr. Jones entered and shook Attilio's left hand. They slipped easily into medical lingo, and this immediate connection based on a common language developed quickly into friendship. As soon as the consultation ended, the young doctor assured his Italian colleague that it was possible to save not only the arm, but also some of the fingers.

According to the beautiful Sicilian secretary who had greeted them so warmly, it would take quite some time before his operation could be scheduled. There was a long list of patients waiting for the famous surgeon to return. "However," she said, "one never knows when a patient may cancel out. Give me your telephone number, and I will keep you informed of any change."

The two left the hospital in high spirits. Things were proceeding quickly. They celebrated at a restaurant whose specialty was fish, a food that they preferred above all others. After a satisfying meal, they caught the train home and with cocktails in their hands, enjoyed the panoramas passing by their windows.

Grace was busy preparing dinner on New Year's Eve when the telephone rang.

"Hello, this is Dr. Edgeton's office. May I speak to Dr. Fazio, please?"

Grace motioned to Attilio that the call was for him, but Attilio replied, "Please, take the message, because my English is limited."

His hostess graciously complied. "May I take the message, please?"

"Tell Dr. Fazio that he will be operated on Monday and that he should come tonight."

"Can you go tonight, Attilio?" Grace called to her guest. "Yes, I can."

Grace spoke into the phone. "Yes, he will be there

tonight. Thank you."

"The good Sicilian secretary must have worked hard to make the miracle happen," Attilio said. "I am sorry to have to leave you, seeing how much preparation you have made to celebrate New Year together. But, really, I didn't think it was going to happen so quickly."

Frank accompanied his friend on the train again, and in three hours they were in the hospital, where they separated, Frank returning to Philadelphia. Later, he and Grace learned that the operation had been so successful that the surgeon was able not only to save Attilio's arm, but also to rehabilitate all five fingers.

The two physicians congratulated each other, and after an exchange of addresses the good Dr. Edgeton told Dr. Fazio that the operation had been a courtesy from one colleague to another. He added that if he were to become ill while in Italy, he would call on him to be treated by the hand he had been able to save.

The Italian physician, for that brief stay in Baltimore, felt like a king, his court being composed of many physicians and nurses who participated in his comfort. The recovery proceeded as foreseen, and then a miracle happened. After only three weeks of convalescence, Attilio resumed his practice.

79 In the late 1970s, while Italy declared war on terrorism, Frank declared war on the kind of insidious bigotry that he had encountered with Dr. Smith and the clerk in the St. Louis hotel. Frank was also overly sensitive to inhumanity, as in the case of the restless physician who, knowing that their child was dying, would not leave the house until he had been paid. All these episodes stimulated Frank to double his efforts for a more civil, more correct, and more just society.

Even so, he knew that people could rise above the bias and succeed. He remembered the autobiography of Michael

Musmanno, a boy of Italian descent who went on to become a prosecutor at the Nuremberg trials and who later served as a Supreme Court justice in the Commonwealth of Pennsylvania. Frank recalled one story about Musmanno who, at the age of twelve, fell in love with an Irish girl named Penelope Worthington, who had arrived in America seven months earlier and was now his classmate. Being very timid, young Michael asked his friend Arthur Young to take his love message to Penelope. The judge describes the event with these words. "The next day, while the school bell was ringing, my friend Arthur told me, 'I talked to Penelope and she said she loves you; she thinks you are wonderful and smart; and she likes to listen to you talk. But she says she can never marry you, because you are a foreigner.' I was born in America; she had been here seven months. She was an American and I was a foreigner!"

This was the environment in which the children of Italian immigrants, in order to be accepted, had to demonstrate that they were model citizens. They had to be twice as capable as the so-called "true Americans" in order to compete.

"When will it end?" Frank asked himself. His grandfather had been a victim of discrimination in the nineteenth century, then his father in the early part of the twentieth century, and now himself. He considered the possibility, however remote, that one day, in the twenty-first century, his own children could be victims of the same discrimination.

Still, Frank was convinced that the American experiment was generally working well and that people of different ethnic groups drew so much energy from each other that assimilation was possible. This *modus operandi* also allowed them to keep their own identity. Many Italians retained time-honored family traditions that centered around such things as religion, language, food, music, and sports. Frank's high-school teachers Nolfi, Zarrella, and Conti treasured their heritage, declaring themselves culturally Italian in this land of Anglo-Saxon traditions.

80

John F. Kennedy was universally regarded as a man of great ideals. The entire country had drawn hope from his doctrine the "New Frontier." Indeed, the destiny of the world seemed to be in his hands. While in Berlin, he sent people into a frenzy by declaring, "*Ich bin ein Berliner*" ("I am a native Berliner"). And then he was killed, and America went through a deep crisis. Every year it seemed to be participating in a funeral for one of its leaders.

The blacks did not yet feel free from the chains of slavery. Many theaters, restaurants, buses, rest rooms, swimming pools, and schools were still segregated.

Small militant groups of activists, black and white, often demonstrated in front of the White House. People feared going out at night. Thousands of young Americans, including many university students, began following various psychedelic groups whose messages were of little value. Many took to the streets to voice their frustration. The police could not cope with the alarming episodes, so the National Guard had to intervene to stop the demonstrations and chants of "no to racism and the war in Vietnam." The angry voices of black civil-rights activists and anti-Vietnam War demonstrators provoked strong violence. Entire neighborhoods in big cities such as Philadelphia, Los Angeles, and Chicago were set ablaze. It seemed as if the old anarchy was replacing the young and fragile democracy. The ideology of hate was clearly manifested on public transportation and on the walls of public buildings where one could see such epithets as "Blacks to lynching" or "Jews to oven."

In spite of the unrest, Frank promoted several cultural and social programs and organizations in his school, including one called Young Italy (*La Giovane Italia*), which became a source of Italian activities for the community, including performances of singing or dancing at local universities and Italian organizations. The female members of Young Italy were invited to serve as cheerleaders for the Italian national basketball team, which arrived in America to challenge the team of Saint Joseph University, a Jesuit institution. Frank's cheerleaders, dressed in red sweaters, white skirts, and green stockings, amused the audience with their cheers in Italian.

Frank also encouraged his students to become involved in the community by giving a hand to the less fortunate, for example, at the Don Guanella School for Handicapped Children, managed by Italian priests. The architect of this village was Frank's compatriot Don Pietro Tullio, affectionately called Father Peter. The good father had created for these unlucky boys a world completely Italian. The roads, the buildings, the fountains all had Italian names, and the parrot in the father's office welcomed people in Italian. He accomplished some wonders with the boys, including the formation of a fine orchestra. Nobody could understand how he had done it, or how he had taught his charges to sing in Italian.

Young Italy spent every Halloween with these children, from six to twenty years of age. They celebrated the holiday with an Italian meal and danced to the sound of Italian music in a festive, ghostly setting, complete with illuminated pumpkins, bloody bats, and witches. There was even the usual jolly cry of "trick or treat."

Over the years Frank extended his Italian program to four years of study, the same level as the other languages—French, Latin, Spanish, and German—that were being taught. His program became so popular that the administration had to hire another full-time teacher.

In 1975 he was named "Italian Teacher of the Year" by the American Institute for Italian Culture and the American Association of Teachers of Italian, which honored him in a special ceremony in which Italian teachers from the Greater Philadelphia area participated. The Consul-General of Italy was one of the many dignitaries. The following year he was named head of the department of foreign languages at Haverford High School.

That same year, Philadelphia and surrounding counties celebrated the bicentennial of the birth of the United States. Frank, as a patriotic American, seized the opportunity to have interested foreign-language students participate by researching historical facts.

However, Frank's main focus was on informing his own students about Italy's role in the history and civilization of the world, with special emphasis on America, their country.

81

In 1978 Frank received a Fulbright grant to the University for Foreigners, in Perugia, where, for forty days, he joined Italian colleagues from all over the world in doing research to establish a film library for scholastic use by both American and Canadian teachers of Italian. At the end, he presented his work to a group of experts from the Ministry of Education in Rome.

One day Dr. Salvatore Castiglione, the school director, asked Frank to organize a friendly soccer game between university professors and the foreign colleagues attending the university. Frank succeeded in getting the names of twelve foreign teachers, but on the day of the game the two Arab teachers were not present. Nevertheless, the game was played in spite of fewer men. For days Frank looked for his Arab colleagues, thinking that they might have been sick. An Egyptian professor later confessed to him that the two had left the university, believing Frank to be an FBI agent.

Horrified at the thought of a possible encounter with incipient terrorism, Frank returned immediately to his apartment and wasted no time ensuring the safety of his wife and children. He took them back to his native village, where his parents had been living in peace with his entire family since their return from the United States. It was a providential move, for Frank saw his father for the last time. A few days later, Joseph Salvato died.

While Grace dedicated much time to preparing their children for

82 spiritual principles that she herself had absorbed from her forefathers, Frank concerned himself with the linguistic education of his children. When Frank took his family on vacation to Chiavari, where Iuccio and Angela had retired, the Tottis noticed immediately that Linda and Richard, now eighteen and fifteen years old respectively, acted responsibly and understood Italian rather well. The two youths revived in Iuccio an old nostalgia for his four grandchildren, Italo's children.

"How I would like to see again my grandchildren! They, too, must be so tall and well behaved."

"All four are tall," Frank reported, "especially the first one, your namesake. He is six feet tall and very smart. Knowing Italo and your daughter-in-law, Pat, I am certain that they keep an eye on all four of them twenty-four hours a day."

"Young people must be checked on every day because in America there are big drug problems that don't exist here," Grace said.

"Even here the drug problems are starting to worry parents," responded Angela.

"Maybe it is true," said Frank, "but here the cases are still sporadic, while in our country, the Flower Generation, born in the sixties, lives on dreams and hopes."

Frank was bothered by an observation he had made earlier and wanted Iuccio's opinion on it, since he had been living in Italy for some time. "Listen," he began, "am I wrong or is there an atmosphere of anti-Americanism here? Did not America save Europe and the rest of the world, during the first and second world conflicts, through humanitarian aid such as the Marshall Plan?"

Frank loved the infinite space of America that stretched "from the mountains, to the prairies, to the ocean." But he also loved its democratic institutions and its spirit of identifying itself with the "underdogs."

"By Jove," Iuccio answered, "Italy has gone communist. Here they all see red like toros do in the streets of Pamplona. The

Communist Party is the second largest in Italy, and it is brainwashed by Moscow. If you analyze the textbooks used by middle schools, high schools and universities, if you look at the newspapers and cultural centers, you will find that everything is tinted red. Have you ever looked at the graffiti in the cities? They are all red. Even the airports and the train stations are red, except that these are stained with human blood. The terrorists did that. Italy, dear Frank, is going through some terrible times."

Frank shook his head. "My question alluded to other important things."

"To what are you referring?"

"Well, for example, I am not sure whether my friends here are serious or whether they are teasing when they say that the Americans discriminate against blacks—as if we emigrants participate in this racism. They come to me with certain stories. As immigrants, we had to swallow this type of prejudice for years in America, working very hard fighting its discriminatory practices. Also, they hate America for the influx of English words into their language, for the useless substitution of English terms only to appear fashionable. Whose fault is that?"

Iuccio thought for a few moments before replying, "Really, I believe that the media—TV and newspapers—have created this linguistic vandalism."

Frank decided to confess something else that was bothering him. "I can understand the importance of English as technical language, but, culturally, we have always exported our language. It is clear that to evolve, a language must continue to digest foreign words when necessary. Nevertheless, I like '*va bene*' better than 'OK.' One may seem less practical than the other, but the first one has a noble sound, while the other has the flavor of a boxer. Too often English words become just auditory jokes, especially for those who don't know English well, and these Italians seem to corrupt our language like the Goths, the Visigoths and the Huns once did. Take the word '*scampagnata*' which is being replaced by the word 'picnic'. The first may be a bit longer, but it gives out fragrance, while the other is odorless.

Iuccio agreed and gestured backward with his hands, signifying that it all belonged to the past. "The English language is contaminating our society, not only with terminology, but also with attitudes."

Frank didn't feel that he had made his point clear. He continued complaining to Iuccio that many beautiful Italian melodies are no longer heard on the radio, because they have been replaced by American music. He was also distressed that he could buy a souvenir T-shirt here on which was written "Beautiful Italy" instead of "*Bella Italia*." According to Iuccio, that was because "Italians accept everything. Resisting fashion trends takes too much effort."

Frank shook his head in dismay.

"You are absolutely right in what you've been saying," Iuccio said. "Italian apathy doesn't allow Italians to understand the problems we Italian-Americans faced as immigrants. I know that young people like you have been promoting positive images and actively combating abuses and negative portrayals of Americans of Italian descent. And you personally are contributing to the economy of Italy, bringing students here instead of to other countries."

Iuccio, though a bit tired, still wanted to let out more steam. "There are many things I regret not having done in America. The one that bothers me the most is not having learned a word of English. Had I learned English, I might not be in Italy now." In America he had lived in an Italian enclave where few felt the need to learn English.

"What are you complaining about?" said Frank. "You are like the Pope in Vatican City—you are in your own home!"

Iuccio smiled, thinking that perhaps it was so. "I was never able to talk to my daughter-in-law. She is a jewel of woman, the daughter of a good Irish family, whose ancestors have lived in Maine for generations. But what pains me most is that I have never had the satisfaction of talking to any of my four grandchildren, even though I lived so many years in that land. I always spoke Italian at home—and on the job, too, because everyone was Italian. When my first granddaughter got married, I was not able to utter a word to her husband, who was also from a very nice Irish family."

Frank always used a positive approach when answering Iuccio, especially about delicate matters, because Iuccio tended to undervalue his intelligence due to his English language deficiency.

"The most important thing today is that everyone gets along well in a family," Frank said. "By the way, did you know that about seventy percent of Italian marriages are with Anglo-Saxon ethnic groups today? Who knows if my grandchildren will speak Italian? This situation is creating an identity crisis, but in the long run it will not be negative. With this fusion of ethnic groups, there is a positive side—less discrimination. The truth is that the Irish and Italians are the two groups who most intermarry."

Iuccio nodded. "Our nationality may decrease, but it will never disappear, because it is an integral part of the soul and body of America."

Frank paused for a few seconds to reflect about the future of the second or even third generations of Italian-Americans. Will they be accepted in the mainstream? Or will they be seen as strangers yet? Finally he said: "Actually, many Italian names that were changed got botched in the translation—for example, Pietro Parchette became Pieter Purkett. But nobody anglicizes names anymore, because Italians are too proud and their children often return to Italy to find their identity again."

Judging from Iuccio's tired expression and his tendency to lose his train of thought, Frank found himself hard-pressed to pursue the conversation. And he was concerned about Iuccio, especially when Iuccio suddenly perked up and announced, "I should be happy because I am home, but I am not. I don't understand what is happening to me."

Frank regarded Iuccio with tenderness. Old age was pursuing his friend with all the afflictions and vicissitudes of

Father Time and tormenting him relentlessly. It was as if the only goal of old age were to hinder him from living a peaceful life in that small heaven to which he had returned.

Frank knew that nearly all immigrants suffer from the same malady, a strange phenomenon that prevents them from enjoying two paradises at once. Having lived in the paradise of America, Iuccio found that his old paradise of Italy did not look quite the same. Iuccio complained about everything: physicians, hospitals, public services, and even magistrates who, according to him, paid more attention to playing politics than to rendering justice. But his complaining was due to nostalgia for his one remaining son and all his grandchildren.

83 Perhaps the nostalgia was too great for Iuccio, for he and Angela did make arrangements to participate in the wedding of Anna, their granddaughter. All their dear ones were waiting in Philadelphia, where they landed for a long visit: Italo, his wife, Pat, their children and families, and Frank and Grace. Turning to Italo, who was standing near his father, Frank asked, "What's your father doing? What is he saying?"

"He bent down to kiss the ground, and he is probably saying the only words he knows in English—God bless America," his cousin answered.

When they greeted each other, Frank saw that Iuccio was wearing the badge that Frank had given him as a gift when he and Angela decided to go back to Italy. It was in the form of two hearts with two flags, symbol of his loyalty to the two countries.

Euphoric days followed and, for a time, tranquillity reigned in the Totti household. But despite the family doctor's sophisticated care, Iuccio began to complain again about his many pains, from the senile degeneration of his legs that no longer let him walk, to the diabetes that prevented him from reading, which had been his passion, to the prolonged use of cortisone that had left his right hand only slightly flexible. And finally, his past nicotine habit aggravated his weak cardiac rhythm. For years he had smoked a few packs of cigarettes a day.

Was it possible that the tender bond with Angela was about to end, after more than a half-century? The more time passed, the more Iuccio lived moments of intense emotions. He became restless, and the music that used to touch the deepest parts of his soul was no longer effective. All the years spent with Angela seemed now as brief as a breath of air. The old lion seemed to walk slowly toward his final destination. The medicines served only to lessen the pains of the accursed malady of the century, cancer.

On the day of his granddaughter's wedding, he was unable to get up from the bed, and his only comfort was the bride and groom's unexpected visit to his bedside. They kissed him tenderly and he gave them his benediction. The physicians' efforts were not able to do much for him, and he expired that evening.

From the day of the funeral, Angela felt the lack of her eternal companion. Strange was the fact that his shadow seemed more real than when he was alive. What comforted her, however, was the thought that Iuccio's last chapter, even if painful, had been brief. She understood clearly that he had been her only source of joy, the craftsman of the fable that for many years had been her existence. She felt especially proud of him for becoming a man in his land of adoption, where his heart was ennobled with the work of his own unprepared hands, ransoming in his own way the honor of his restless and imprudent lifestyle. Her face, slightly wrinkled, still showed the beauty of her youth that puberty had anticipated for her, and it reflected the love that had been in her life with him.

84 Frank's mother, Maria, died at the beautiful age of ninety-six. Excluding Grace, she had been the person whom Frank had loved and admired the most. Her death caused Frank to withdraw from

active life for a while, but Grace's common sense and abundant affection helped to ease his grief in the same fashion that Toro, his peaceful native village, had made his ulcers disappear many years before. Eventually he was able to re-focus on his educational mission.

Frank knew well the Italian-American mentality and character. If the first to arrive had been in a hurry to dissociate from the language and culture of their forefathers, their grandchildren understood the importance of rediscovering their noble roots.

In the last phase of what had been his mission, Frank succeeded in starting other studies of Italian. One was at Lamberton High School in West Philadelphia, and the other at the Philadelphia College of Pharmacy and Science in the same city. Satisfied that he had accomplished much, Frank and Grace regained some regularity in their lives and were preparing to enjoy a rather simple life during that final stage of their life as retirees. President Thomas Jefferson said that we have the right to aim for happiness, but that to get it, we need to work hard. Frank and Grace had worked vigorously, reaching many objectives, devoting themselves day and night to educating their children. Despite their many disappointments, they had built their children's ethical spirit little by little, stone by stone, like the construction of a house. Therefore, they were preparing to rediscover the pleasure and the freedom of their own youth.

They planned long vacations in the most familiar places, such as Atlantic City, a place where they could relive their honeymoon. Above all, they planned to return to Frank's village, a place of so many beautiful memories—from the unusual sound of the church bell, to the echoes of known voices, to the barking of dogs late at night.

For Grace, too, returning to Toro was almost like going home. She had left her jovial, democratic, American imprint on the daily life of the village. She was esteemed and admired, not only by her peers, but also by all those who came in contact with her. Clearly, she had a passion for that pristine life. She had such sensibility, always remembering to bring everyone a little memento. She was generous, especially with children, even if it was just a package of American chewing gum, for it was so different from Italian gum.

She would often start conversing with her mother-in-law's illiterate friends as she sat with them in front of their homes, a gesture which demonstrated her immense kindness and respect for them. She and Frank were happy. They were among many friends.

For the Salvatos, Christmas of 1998 promised to be special. Their son Richard was coming home from Reno, Nevada, where snow could be seen almost all year round, and bringing with him his fiancée, Lisa, and her parents. Richard's sister, Linda, had just crossed the United States from Los Angeles to Philadelphia in three days, soloing in her small Piper airplane, and would be coming with her fiancé, Terry Berl, from Wilmington, Delaware. Frank had re-created a nativity scene, but had given it much more detail than in previous years. However, a winter storm blanketed the Philadelphia area with two feet of snow, preventing airplanes from landing there and forcing the Salvatos to postpone their first meeting with their future relatives.

In the late winter Grace began preparing for the summer's trip to Europe. "Frank, do you like this blouse I bought today?" she would say. Every day she came home with purchases: sweaters, suits, and shoes for the long walks they expected to take on their trip. Frank put the wheels in motion, and within a month all the nephews, relatives and friends across the ocean knew the date of their proposed arrival. A Sunday did not go by without calling Italy to update everyone about their travel plans.

Sunday, April 18, began as a marvelous day; the sky was clear, the trees were in bloom, and the birds were chirping behind the Salvatos' home. Grace got up to make some espresso as she had done every day of her conjugal life. Frank went down to the kitchen, embracing her and wishing her a happy birthday. He then presented her with lilies, her favorite flower, which she put in a vase, while Linda fussed with a bracelet she had bought for her mother. A little later, Grace's brother, Tony, called her from Ohio and with his wife, Lucy, wished her a happy birthday. Finally came the call from Richard, who was practicing law in Nevada. For Grace the day was complete, and her joy was revealed in her serene eyes and on her still youthful face.

For a moment Frank felt that there had been a short circuit between the two of them. He had had an uneasy premonition, but her cheerful face reassured him. About twelve o'clock Grace developed a hammering headache, as she described it. And then she fainted. While Linda was trying to comfort her mother, she asked her panic-stricken father to call 911. With heroic efforts, Linda immediately started mouth-to-mouth resuscitation on her lifeless mother. The ambulance arrived five minutes later, and in ten minutes the three were in the hospital. After a proper diagnosis the physicians advised them to take her to Wills Eye Hospital in Philadelphia, where surgeons immediately operated on her for a brain aneurysm. She remained in a coma for a week.

Frank and Linda, and now Richard, who had come immediately upon learning of the needed operation, waited for six days with their hearts in tumult, seeing their rose withering away. On the seventh day they were in the waiting room at the hospital when the young doctor asked them to follow him into his office. After a brief but emotionally wrenching explanation, he informed them, "There is little hope. Grace belongs to the dark vegetable world, and we only need to turn off the light."

"Doctor, please, explain to us in simple terms what is happening," pleaded Frank.

"Death is not very complicated when it arrives," the physician answered.

The news was even more shocking because the previous evening had given them reason to hope. Frank, Linda, and Richard had gone home from the hospital breathing their first sigh of relief. For the first time in a week since Grace's operation, she had been able to breathe without the help of a machine.

"But, Doctor," Frank persisted, "last night you gave us hope that…"

The physician interrupted him. "But we did not succeed in keeping the cranial pressure under control. It seemed that the operation for the aneurysm in the brain had succeeded. But you may put a match under her feet, and she will not feel any burning. I am sorry."

For Frank, the world without Grace's ingenuity and good judgment would be too complicated and less virtuous. Now her fragile life was passing before them, fading like a rainbow at a storm's end.

Nevertheless, Frank and his children clung to hope. Then Frank had an idea. He knew that acoustic and optic stimulations stirred memory. He knew that music was capable of reawakening the consciousness. So he proposed to bring in a tape of music recorded in Toro, her adopted village, music that she had liked more than any other. He wanted to bring to her, from that faraway world, the sound of those bells and the voices of dear relatives and friends. Instead, Grace, his love, arrived at the moment of truth without resistance. She slept quietly, peacefully, just as he had seen her do many other evenings when she had gone to sleep with a book in her hands. And he would later turn off the light in the depth of her sleep.

Now the aneurysm was causing her to become a fading rose. Frank didn't want to believe that his world was about to collapse. He could not let himself believe it. He didn't believe it. It was not true. It was just a terrible nightmare.

While the nurse was removing all the tubes that sustained her, her soul was slipping away, a bit at a time, without anybody fully realizing it. Frank and his children embraced. Then, while Linda and Richard held Grace's right hand, Frank held her left, as if they could stop her from dying by holding on, at least for a little while, just to have a last chance to tell her how much they loved her.

Linda, meanwhile, was looking at the monitor, at the visible rhythm of that heart which had lavished so much love on her and which was now weakening more and more. When she heard her father call "Grace" for the last time, Linda began to cry uncontrollably. Then the three embraced again, lightly including her, forming one body, almost as though they were trying to leave this world with her. Grace had reached that quietude suggested by the prophetic words she had often repeated: "When the time comes, let it be suddenly."

85 The people, elbow to elbow in church, incredulous, shocked, kept shaking their heads sorrowfully, remembering Grace's simplicity, generosity, and kindness. Angela, flanked by Italo and his wife, still strong even after so many storms in her life, could not control her emotions and cried continually. Linda and Richard, both numb, were remembering their mother's endless love.

Every few seconds, Frank's mind was invaded by flashing images that took him back to his childhood: playing soccer in the narrow streets of his neighborhood; World War II with its misery, its hunger; the dolorous departure from his village; the crossing of the ocean; the discovery of heaven in his adopted country; the many doubts he started to have, and Grace's encouragement; the wedding; his small children observing the Mysteries in Campobasso, with their wide-open eyes; the death of his son and of Benjamin, Iuccio, his parents. Now the one who had been the passport to a happy life, his love, was lying in front of him, a photograph of a radiantly smiling Grace placed on her casket. It didn't seem possible that death could ever separate them.

Fortune seemed to have turned its back on Frank. The life he knew with Grace had been swept away from him like a seed in a hurricane, lost in the ferocity of the wind. Though small and fragile, she had been his guide and strength for fifty-three years, most of his life.

86 Frank's children went back to work, but for him the world stood still. His mind was deadened like a flower after a long drought. He felt lonely and lifeless without Grace. His dog and cat were his only company. He tried to give his full attention to all the affectionate messages from relatives and friends, perhaps a hundred of them. Their words were wise and pleasant, but they could not fill the abyss created by her absence. His every thought returned to her, his only love. His memories of the past, which united him perpetually with her, were his only comfort. Her shadow was always present, especially in his dreams, for which he now treasured the nights. The days were too painful.

He wanted to avoid embarrassing scenes with people, but often he felt like caving in to the overwhelming urge to cry. Instead, he bit his lips to forestall tears. He wanted to cry, but the circumstances dictated a more appropriate behavior. But when he was alone at home or in the places where they had taken their daily early-morning walks or in their car—even the license plate, Toro CB, reminded him of her because it had been her idea—he cried his heart out. Friends suggested that he seek peace at church, but since the death of little Frankie long ago, Frank had been unable to pray.

Grace had been the first to reveal to Frank the secrets of that sweet, yet bitter America, which treated the children of Italian descent as its own when the time came to go to war, yet sent their parents to concentration camps. She had always made herself available to welcome immigrants, alerting them to the Dr. Jekyll/Mr. Hyde nature of their new homeland, a place that could be hostile but which also had the capacity for great hospitality and goodness. Still, this magnificent country had attracted millions of people from all over the world in their search for freedom. At times they may have felt that they were at the edge of an abyss, but mostly their spirit and hope rose to levels never seen elsewhere on the face of the earth. Did all of this matter, now that the sun had gone down? Perhaps it did ultimately.

Does it matter if the lantern went out?
If its oil is burned out?
It has made light.
Does it matter if the carnation
Has bent and has faded?
It gave out fragrance.
Does it matter if the grain of wheat
Is dragged away by the ant?
It has been food.

Grace would have answered Frank with a poem she knew well:

Do not stand by my grave and weep.
I am not there. I do not sleep.
I am the thousand winds that blow,
I am the diamond glints on the snow,
I am the sunlight on the ripened grain.
And in the morning's silent hush,
I am the stars that shine at night.
Do not stand by my grave and cry,
I am not there, I did not die.

87 It was June 18, 1998, exactly two months after Grace's last birthday, the day of the annual Delaware County Senior Games for 55-year-olds and older. The sky was clear, with an ideal temperature of 76 degrees. At the last moment a friend with whom Frank had competed in the past implored and finally convinced him to participate. In a sense he entered the contest almost in defiance of Death, which had stolen his love from him. He had not prepared for this year's races; he had not done any kind of training, as he had in preceding years when he went on to win some gold medals. He had not even warmed up.

He ran first in the 100-yard competition, losing it to a

contemporary who finished in 15 seconds, beating Frank by one second. Then he participated in the men's mile run, coming in second again. His failures discouraged him, and he was a little resentful of the teasing he received for wearing a shirt with the image of the Italian flag. Nevertheless, he decided to take one last chance, one last try in the most difficult competition, the 5K, a three-mile run that he was used to winning.

As that race progressed, Frank never lost sight of the leader. After a while Frank began sweating profusely, soaking through his clothes. Under the wet, tri-colored shirt another flag clearly revealed itself—the Stars and Stripes. At that same moment the spectators began to cheer for him. Encouraged by the applause, he made his move during the last two hundred yards and overtook his rival to come in first at the finish line. Everyone congratulated him. Upon receiving the medal, he kissed it and looked up toward the sky, saying to himself, "Cara, you helped me one last time to win."

JANUS

88 Encouraged by his children, Frank decided to return to his native village for a while, attracted by his childhood memories and by the town's antiquities. There he could still enjoy the splendor of a sunset that hasty people didn't see, the desired peace that only expatriates can discover.

He tried to "escape" in Italy, but he cried when he remembered the first time he had brought Grace there. Tears welled up when he saw the church where she had prayed and where her sisters-in-law had convinced her to prepare Linda for her first Communion. They had dressed Linda like an angel with wings, as if she were ready to fly. He could almost picture the scene after the ceremony when, as soon as she came out of the church, they all lined up to kiss her and wish her the best. He tearfully remembered his father as he removed his hat in reverence and love for his granddaughter and kissed her first, followed by her grandmother and all the others.

It is said that time heals all wounds. Gradually, Frank realized that although his pain would lessen, there would always remain a scar. Still, one can survive with scars, and so he determined to adjust to his "new normal." He would continue to enjoy some of the pleasures that he and Grace had shared, and for balance in his existence, he would return to Havertown, where they had spent most of their life together, and try to open his heart to new experiences.

About the Author

Frank Salvatore emigrated to the United States in 1947 from his native Italy where he had been attending high school in Campobasso. He continued his studies in Youngstown, Ohio, and went on to graduate from Youngstown State University with a B.A. degree in Spanish. In addition to mastering English, he became proficient in Spanish, attending the Escuela de Verano in Mexico and eventually receiving an M.A. degree in Spanish from the prestigious Middlebury College, in Middlebury, Vermont.

He has spent most of his teaching career in Pennsylvania. For almost thirty years, he was a teacher of foreign languages at Haverford High School and is now an instructor at Villanova University.

Frank Salvatore has received many honors, including a Fulbright grant to pursue research at the University of Perugia in Italy. He is a past president of the American Association of Teachers of Italian and is a member of the American Association of Teachers of Spanish and Portuguese.

A widower with two grown children, a son and a daughter, he now makes his home in Havertown, Pennsylvania.

This is his first book.